Sto.

)

# RED CURTAIN UP

1. In *Swan Lake* at the Bolshoi.

*Beryl Grey*

# Red Curtain Up

DODD, MEAD & COMPANY   *New York*

TO SVEN—MY HUSBAND

# CONTENTS

## Part One

### MY RUSSIAN TOUR

## Part Two

### THE SOVIET BALLET

All but seven of the photographs were taken by the author's husband, Dr S. G. Svenson, with a Leica camera. Nos. 1, 3, 27, 39, 40, 41 and 42 were kindly supplied by the Soviet authorities.

# ILLUSTRATIONS

ILLUSTRATIONS

# *AUTHOR'S NOTE*

THIS IS THE RECORD OF MY IMPRESSIONS DURING four and a half weeks' dancing and travelling in the Soviet Union.

I feel it is important to emphasise that this book does not pretend to be anything more than that. There is no attempt to give any verdict about political or economic conditions because, as the reader will see, I was too occupied to think about much except dancing. There is also no attempt to provide a definitive study of the Soviet ballet, the Bolshoi Theatre, or Soviet ballet personalities. I deal with all these things; but naturally, in view of the shortness of my stay, my experiences were limited.

The book is divided into two parts. The first is a chronological account of my trip, with my personal and spontaneous reactions. The second is a more studied and detailed report of the Soviet ballet as it impressed me.

As I was the first Western ballerina to be invited to dance at the Bolshoi, I hope that what I saw and what I was told will be of interest not only to followers of the ballet but also to all who believe in artistic exchanges between as many countries as possible.

I wish to thank the editor of the *Sunday Times* for permission to include some of the material contained in three articles by me originally published in that newspaper.

# PART ONE

# My Russian Tour

# Chapter I

## *SWAN IN THE SKY*

INSIDE there were lace curtains, the glint of carefully polished brass, the tinkling of tea-things. It was all very much like the Palm Court of some provincial hotel. I should not have been surprised if a fountain had suddenly started playing discreetly in the aisle. Occasionally I drowsed off, and each time I woke it was an effort to realise that I was in a jet airliner travelling towards Moscow at 600 miles an hour.

Yet the idea seemed very natural. After all, I could hardly remember the time when I had not been hoping, somewhere inside me, that one day I should visit Russia. There was nothing political about this feeling. To a serious dancer the Russian ballet is something like Mecca must be to a Moslem. And for twenty-five of my thirty years the study of ballet-dancing has been my chief preoccupation. Now, not only was I going to see the Bolshoi Theatre: I was going to dance there.

So, as we flew on, I clutched a symbolic glass of vodka, and came to the conclusion that I was probably the most excited of the seventy passengers on board—and also the most frightened.

This was the high point of my career so far. I could see a graph-line climbing jerkily upwards until it reached the point, high over Czechoslovakia, where I was sitting in this Russian TU104 airliner and wondering what was going to happen to me during the next five weeks.

But the highest point is also the point from which you have farthest to drop. That was why there was a tight feeling inside me which was not entirely connected with the fact that I am never very happy in an aeroplane.

I knew that when I was in Russia my dancing would be judged

3

by their standards—that is, by the highest standards in the world. I would be a curiosity as well as a ballerina. They had invited me to be the first dancer from the West to appear in a leading role at the Bolshoi. That meant that everything I did, off the stage as well as on, would be studied as through a microscope.

Again I was well aware that not everyone in the Soviet Union was acquainted with the development of British ballet, which by their standards is absurdly young. They were not altogether convinced that it is possible to achieve such a standard of performance without a long tradition.

So they would not only be judging me, but would be assessing through me the quality of British ballet. That was certainly an unnerving thought. So while I was very proud about being invited to Russia, I was also quite shaken.

I am used to this feeling—this combination of exhilaration and tightness. It has been with me all my dancing life. But, except when I have been ill, I do not know a time when the sight and the feel of a stage have not dispelled it all.

I have been dancing since I was four. At first I danced only because I liked it, and because it was an extra subject which I took at school for no particular reason. I found myself passing examinations. They seemed quite easy, and then, suddenly, when I was nine, there were no more examinations which I could take at that age. So my teacher sent me to Sadler's Wells to see what they thought of me. The Sadler's Wells offered me a big surprise, a place in their school.

But my parents could not afford the fees, so that appeared to be that. Then, surprise again, Sadler's Wells offered a four years' scholarship, plus a place in the company with a four years' contract if I developed satisfactorily at the end of my training. So I entered the school in September 1937.

The war began before my training was finished. All the plans made by Dame Ninette de Valois for introducing me gradually to major dancing roles had to be abandoned. At fourteen, after six months in the *corps de ballet*, I was doing leading roles in one-act ballets. In one week, I remember, I had four new roles.

I celebrated my fifteenth birthday by dancing Odette-Odile in *Swan Lake* with Robert Helpmann; by the time I was nineteen I had danced all the leading classical roles except *Coppelia*.

4

Outside the Bolshoi Theatre on my first morning in Moscow.

The auditorium of the Bolshoi Theatre.

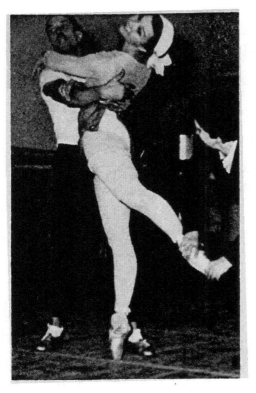

4. Rehearsing with Chaboukiani.
Semeyonova alters a foot position.

5. I meet the Bolshoi *corps de ballet* on s

But how was it that I was travelling to Moscow, alone except for my doctor husband, Sven S.venson? I had been a member of Sadler's Wells—now the Royal Ballet—for twenty years. Early in 1957 I felt the overwhelming urge to break new ground. I wanted to develop my own personality in the wider international field.

I had reached a point in my career when I longed to experiment with my own powers of self-expression, which was not possible while I was a member of a strongly directed company. In short, I wanted to be a ballerina on my own.

The first fruits of this were trips to South and Central America and to South Africa. Both went very well, judging by box-office and criticism. They also proved to me that people in foreign countries were genuinely interested in the British ballet.

For ten weeks I toured Mexico, Argentina, Brazil, Chile, Guatemala, Honduras, and Uruguay. It was a real baptism of fire. I not only had to grapple with differences in temperament and languages, but in the recitals I was also responsible for staging, lighting, and general production.

Then came an entirely different experience during my seven weeks in South Africa. It was a period of fruit and sunshine, and much less harassing than Latin America, as I stayed a minimum of one week in each place, always giving the same two recital programmes.

But all the time I was thinking of Russia. I had been due to go there, of course, with the Sadler's Wells Company in the autumn of 1956. But that trip was cancelled, and when I left the company the following spring no arrangements had been made for a later date.

There had been suggestions that I might be invited to the Soviet Union as the first Western ballerina to dance there. It is difficult to recall when these started.

I had first met Russian dancers in 1954 when Raisa Struchkova and her husband, Alexander Lapauri, were dancing at the Prince's Theatre. My son Ingvar had just been born and, as the Sadler's Wells Company were dancing in Paris, I was one of the few Covent Garden dancers in London. So I was asked to go backstage to make friends with the Russians—and found this was easy.

5

I had seen films of the Russian ballet during the war and had thrilled to them then. Now I was invited to more ballet film shows at the Russian Embassy. Often I was told: "It would be so nice if you could dance in the Soviet Union."

Later, the suggestions became more direct. They said: "You are being invited." And by the time I came back from South Africa all had been settled.

The financial arrangements were generous. The trip was to last four weeks and would include performances in Moscow, Leningrad, and Kiev. The ballets in which I would appear were to be *Swan Lake* and *Giselle*. It was difficult, though, to obtain any other details; it was only shortly before I left that I knew who my partner was to be.

I was delighted when I heard he would be Vachtang Chaboukiani, one of the most famous dancers in the Soviet Union, who has been decorated three times for his dancing and directs the ballet company in Tiflis.

Visas were another difficulty. We could not leave London until our passports had been stamped, but, though all the travel arrangements had been made, we could not get the visas. We were due to leave on Friday, December 6th; it was not until the afternoon of December 4th that we actually got them.

Our start was not very promising. We were held up for hours at London Airport by fog—the same fog in which the terrible railway disaster at Lewisham took place. But at last our plane took off, and, after changing at Paris and Prague, we boarded our TU104.

How reassuring it was to have Sven with me! We had met in Chicago in 1949, and were married the following summer in England. Since then he has done everything possible to help me in my career. So when the invitation included him, he could not resist the temptation. Leaving his practice for a month, we flew off together.

It was in the TU104 that I had the first chance to practise my Russian. Three Soviet citizens, who had travelled on the same aeroplanes from London, got into conversation with us, and it was cheering to find out that they had heard all about my visit.

I had been going to the Berlitz School in London almost every other day for more than a month in an attempt to learn something of the language of the country in which I was going to dance.

6

Sven was very surprised when at my first try I seemed to understand what was being said to me. So was I!

I had prepared for the visit in other ways as thoroughly as possible. I had seen the wonderful film of the Bolshoi Company's *Giselle* several times to mark the differences in choreography; and, of course, I had worked hard at my dancing. For six weeks I had spent four or five hours every day at the studio of my teacher, Audrey de Vos, in Notting Hill Gate, and I had had new costumes made. As I sat in the airliner I ran over all these things and decided that, whatever happened, I had done as much as I could do personally to make certain that my visit would not be a failure.

My first Russian meal was odd but satisfying. The airport building at Prague had smelt too much of sausages and beer to provoke my appetite, but now I found I was hungry and was pleased to see the tray containing meat loaf, *sauté* potatoes, dill pickle, black and white bread, sweet biscuits, and Russian tea with lemon, which the stewardess gave me.

But I am not a good flyer. Soon my ears were hurting too much for me to take any pleasure in seeing the lights of Russia which appeared beneath us as the airliner came down to land.

The landing was typical of many which I was to make all over the Soviet Union. The plane seemed suddenly to dive at the earth —and there we were, with our wheels running along the ground.

My first real sight of Russian territory was from the aircraft steps as I paused for a moment and saw the bright red star gleaming over the snow-covered tarmac and illuminating the airport name-sign.

We were greeted by correspondents from Reuter's and the *Daily Worker*, but there was nobody from the Bolshoi to meet me— quite a disappointment. However, there were waiting a representative from the Ministry of Culture and an attractive blonde girl who said she was to be my interpreter. I was touched to find that the British Ambassador, Sir Patrick Reilly, had sent one of those charming young men that only the Foreign Office can produce to take me into Moscow in an Embassy car.

But the Ministry of Culture man wouldn't hear of this, and soon we were going along in his big black Zim on the twenty-mile drive into Moscow, speeding past snow-clad fields and bare-looking birch trees, past the new skyscraper university, past what

7

seemed to be a five-mile-long housing project, until we came into the city—brightly lit, I thought, but with very few cars.

And then we were passing the Red Square, floodlit and looking like a stage set, with more red stars gleaming from the Kremlin towers. Suddenly we were passing the Bolshoi itself. It too was floodlit and a beautiful sight. I found myself praying that my performances would be good.

We were to stay at the Hotel Metropole and I found this was, like the Bolshoi, in Sverdlov Square. It gave me a comforting feeling to think that I should be sleeping so close to the theatre.

The Metropole was huge and cavernous. The carpets in the corridors and on the stairs were covered with drugget. Desks and tables were under dust-sheets, as they were every night. The *décor* was all very Edwardian.

We were trailing along the corridor to our room—the Ministry of Culture man, my interpreter, Sven, and myself—when we were greeted by an English voice. It was Terence Lancaster, the *Daily Express* staff reporter in Moscow, who had been prevented from meeting us at the airport because he had had to go to a big diplomatic reception where Mr Krushchev had made a speech.

He had come out to report the fortieth anniversary celebrations on November 7th, and was staying on to arrange a top-level interview between his editor, Edward Pickering, and Mr Krushchev. In four weeks he had become quite an old Moscow hand, and we saw a great deal of him during the nine days we were in Moscow.

He took us down to the main dining-room, and on to the kitchens, where we made a desperate effort to order prunes and toast and marmalade for our breakfast next morning. Then we went back to our rooms. We had a large sitting-room with a dining-table and, in a curtained annexe, a double bedroom, with a bathroom leading off. The furniture seemed comfortable but heavy.

Then came the second disappointment. The Ministry of Culture man told us that it had been decided to cut Leningrad from our tour and substitute Tiflis. I quite liked the idea of going to Tiflis, but I was distressed at the possibility of missing Leningrad. I wanted so much to see and dance in the great Maryinsky Theatre, and I said so, quite forcefully. I put forward an alternative plan: either miss Tiflis or cut down our stay there, and still go on to

8

Leningrad. That got no response from the Ministry of Culture, but I resolved to take it up the next morning.

We had a brief meal in our room: I only wanted tea with lemon, and some fruit, but Sven had caviare as well. I had already discovered that the bath water was almost cold. I was tired out, my ears were aching again, I had seen nobody from the Bolshoi yet, and I was not going to Leningrad. My first few hours in Russia had not been very satisfactory. I crawled into bed and resolved that from now on things must go better. At once I fell asleep.

Chapter II

## BEHIND THE BOLSHOI FAÇADE

THE bath water was still cold next morning, but somehow it didn't seem to matter so much. I was anxious to see Moscow and, above all, to make contact with the Bolshoi people.

But a lot was to happen before I managed to do that. First came breakfast—and the prunes and marmalade which I had ordered so confidently the night before turned out to be plums in syrup and a curious sort of strawberry jam. Sven asked for eggs and bacon, but his eggs were a little liquid by Western standards, and the bacon was pieces of ham cooked in with the eggs.

However, we had good Russian tea, and I had brought a pot of marmalade for emergencies like this, and it went well with the toast and the excellent black bread.

Our interpreter of the night before turned up as arranged at about 11.30 a.m. She was named Jhana Feodotova, and stayed with us for the rest of the trip. She was smartly dressed—she told us later she had had clothes made specially for this job—and was an attractive, fair-haired girl who had a journalist husband and a two-year-old baby. She confided that this was her first big assignment for the Ministry of Culture.

Her English was excellent and she was always as charming and helpful as possible. However, she tended to be defeated from time to time by the fact that it was difficult to obtain any travel tickets in the Soviet Union until the last possible moment. The result was that she spent a great deal of time waiting about away from us, and we spent a great deal of time waiting about for Jhana!

We were impatient to leave the hotel, for the sun was shining, there was a layer of crisp snow over Sverdlov Square, and the dry cold seemed to give a tingle to the whole of life.

10

I wanted to see the chief sights, and Sven, who is interested in photography, wanted to use his Leica. So there was no discussion about how we were to spend the morning.

First, of course, came the Red Square, which seemed to me a placid version of Whitehall and Parliament Square and Oxford Street rolled into one. Besides the Kremlin, it contains St Basil's Cathedral, the Lenin-Stalin mausoleum, and Gum, the leading department store. Sven shot picture after picture while I gazed at the gilded loveliness of St Basil's, peered through the Kremlin gates, and watched one of the most impressive sights of our trip— about three thousand people queueing for hours in the cold in order to spend a few minutes inside the mausoleum. They were like the crowds I remembered waiting during the lying-in-state of our own King George VI, and I was told the Red Square queues had been one of the sights of Moscow for more than thirty years.

Then we drove down to Sverdlov Square again and I got out and stood in front of the Bolshoi. It was a major moment in my life as I touched the famous pillars for the first time. I suppose I should have had forebodings about whether I should manage to uphold the prestige of British ballet. But I am afraid my main sensation was impatience because all the doors were closed, together with anxiety about how soon I could get inside and start working.

Now came a quick trip to the Ministry of Culture. At Jhana's suggestion, we went by Metro. This was spotlessly clean, and as impressive as we had been told it was.

The ministry was in a pleasant house, with a Viennese look about it, in the old quarter of the town. Inside we met Mr Boni, charming but shy, who confessed he had no idea why we were to go to Tiflis, instead of Leningrad, as he had only just returned from Poland! So at the end of our long interview I was still hoping to dance in Leningrad if I could. We heard it suggested as a possible reason for the change that, as two more Western dancers were due in Russia soon, it would perhaps be best to send us to different places. Alternatively, it was hinted that since Chaboukiani, my partner, directed the Tiflis company, it was only courteous for us to go there. But both these facts had been known long before we left London, where we had been promised categorically that I should dance at the Maryinsky.

11

To get back to the hotel we made our first trip by Moscow taxi. These cars have bright green lights shining when they are disengaged, which seems a great improvement on the London flag system, as it means you can spot a free one a good way back.

At the Metropole we ate for the first time downstairs in the hotel's main dining-room. This was rather reminiscent of the main rooms in some of the larger Bloomsbury hotels, only vaster, and its dripping fountain gave it quite a sub-aqueous atmosphere. As we ate caviare I heard an English voice and looked round to find Noel Clark, the former Washington correspondent of the *Daily Mail*, sitting at the next table. He also was most helpful to us during the first days when everything was strange.

Then came the big event. At long last we were inside the Bolshoi. We walked across the square and all the doors which had seemed so permanently closed during the morning were thrown open. At once I had a feeling that I was wanted and expected.

At this juncture, I would like to emphasise my very happy relations with the Soviet dancers and theatre administrators throughout my stay. Sometimes in this book I mention things which occasionally annoyed and frustrated me during the visit. Things go wrong on every foreign tour. But there was never any annoyance or frustration about my association with the Soviet ballet.

From the moment I stepped inside the Bolshoi until the moment I left Russia I felt enfolded by the warmth and care of my fellow-dancers. I was at home from the moment they first greeted me. There was no feeling that we belonged to different nations. I was a dancer. I was to dance with them. That was enough. It meant that I was one of them, and everything possible had to be done to make certain that I should give to the performances the best that was in me.

At the top of the first flight of stairs I was met by a group of people. Among them I recognised instantly Vachtang Chaboukiani. He is a slim, handsome man, with a slight moustache and typical Georgian features. He wondered when I would like to start rehearsing and seemed very relieved when I suggested the following day. I'm sure he was afraid that I wanted to start at once. He had been travelling from Georgia for two days and two nights by train; this would have been quite a strain for him.

First rehearsal on stage with Kondratov.

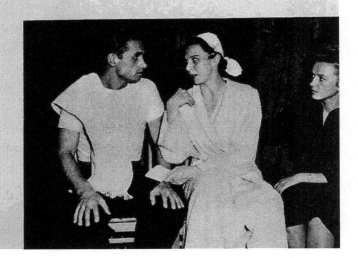

With Kondratov
er rehearsal. Jhana is
erpreting.

8. Last rehearsal with Kondratov before our first night on Sunday, December 15th.

9. Rehearsing me at the Bolshoi. *Left to right:* Marina Semeyonova, Jhana, Asaf Messerer, Yuri Faier, his personal accompanist, and Vera Petrova.

10. Rehearsing on stage with Kondratov and the Kiev Company. The women's practice dresses are longer than at the Bolshoi.

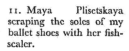

11. Maya Plisetskaya scraping the soles of my ballet shoes with her fish-scaler.

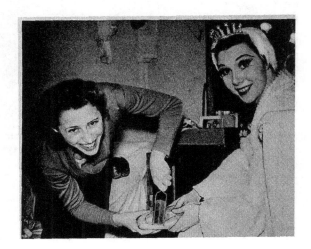

Mikhailov Chulaki, the director of the Bolshoi, was waiting for us in his room. He is large, in some ways like a benevolent teddy-bear, with thick glasses, behind which his eyes smiled a sincere welcome. He had been in England during the Bolshoi visit and so we were old friends. We had grown to like him during our short meetings in London, but it took our visit to Moscow to show us the quiet authority which he used in his own theatre and also the warmth and sincerity of his personality.

I was terribly eager to get the feel of the Bolshoi at once, so we set out on an exploration. We left Mr Chulaki's office—a long, rectangular room, beautifully furnished and quite unlike the cramped quarters of most British administrators—and found ourselves in an atmosphere from which it was possible to guess that in the Soviet Union the ballet people really do get as much as they need.

We received a swift impression of marble staircases, of red carpets, and of red and gold furniture. We went down a flight of steps into the director's box. This was just above stage level, and on the right of the stage as the public looks at it. They put on the lights for us, and for the first time I saw this huge, wonderful theatre, which seats more than 2,000 people. The tiers reminded me of the Colon Theatre in Buenos Aires, it had a hint of the Scala at Milan, and there was also a suggestion of the intimacy of the Metropolitan in New York.

This feeling of intimacy I tried to analyse later. Though the theatre is so large, I personally found it easier to reach the audience there than at Covent Garden. I decided that this was partly due to the height of the proscenium arch, which made me feel I was much nearer the audience, and also to the fact that the stage was raked—but raked in the best possible way, inasmuch as it sloped down towards the footlights but levelled out before it got there. I felt throughout my stay that the rake was perfectly proportioned and balanced.

But on this first occasion the curtain was down and there were many apologies because they could not raise it for me to see the stage from the box. The battens—the top lights—were being washed, so we had to go behind before I could get my first glimpse of this huge stage, which measures 85 feet by 185 feet.

We found the long lines of battens were being cleaned by

women and men, and the stage seemed alive with scores of people. It gave me that sense of being in an active, living theatre which still has the power of thrilling me. I found a space in the middle, and, watched by many curious eyes, I took off my shoes and made a few little jumps. This stage was going to be very important to me. I wanted to get to know it as soon as possible. To my delight it was not at all hard. I could sense that it had all the spring and give a dancer could wish for. I had rather expected that this would be so. Nevertheless, it was a great relief, because to a dancer every stage has a definite personality. This one was going to be all right!

Mr Chulaki left the theatre with us and took us for a short drive round Moscow in his car. Then, after a rest at the hotel, we went to the British Embassy for a small dinner-party with the Ambassador and his wife, Sir Patrick and Lady Reilly.

They sent their Rolls-Royce for us and we found the Embassy was in one of the finest positions in Moscow—just across the river from the floodlit Kremlin. I remember we had a huge bowl of caviare at dinner. I came away with a feeling that my visit was quite appreciated by the British colony in Russia. Another reason for giving the best performances of my life, I told myself.

Sir Patrick and his wife were kindness itself throughout our stay. They told me they had arranged a party for us on Friday night, after my first performance.

Next morning I arrived at the theatre to find the public swarming in. Apparently it is a Moscow custom to give a midday performance in the theatres on Sundays, and that day the Bolshoi Opera Company were performing *The Snow Maiden*.

I was shown to a temporary dressing-room and then went up by lift to the wardrobe, where I found my tu-tu box. I put on my practice tunic—I had been careful to have one resembling the Russian practice tunics made in London before I left.

As I entered the rehearsal-room all the dancers stopped work and greeted me with applause. It reinforced the feeling of welcome I had experienced the previous day and gave me the encouragement I needed at that moment.

At the end of class I started rehearsing with Chaboukiani with the first *pas de deux* in Act II of *Swan Lake*. This is the act in which I first appear. Nothing was exactly the same and I felt the whole

14

business would be hard going. But then the famous ballerina Marina Semeyonova arrived and everything fell into place.

She had been one of the leading exponents of Odette-Odile in *Swan Lake*, and took endless trouble with me. Semeyonova has a wonderfully sympathetic personality and is a magnificent teacher.

I enjoyed working with Chaboukiani. Beneath his humility I was fully conscious of his artistry and great experience. We pushed on slowly, for he had his troubles as well. He had been away from the Bolshoi for six years and his version of *Swan Lake* was the old one. In the interval a new immensely successful version had been staged by the Bolshoi ballet-master Messerer. So there we were with three different versions—the two Bolshoi ones and mine. It was lucky that we had Semeyonova. She helped us enormously in making the right blend, and I was glad to note that our tastes agreed.

Though it was hard work, we managed that first day to rehearse both *pas de deux* in Acts II and III, and the first entrance in Act II. I was dead tired when we got back to the hotel and found the bath water tepid and the shower ice-cold. We ate again in our room— we made a habit of this because of the slow service in the restaurant —and had good caviare and rather disappointing *shashlik*.

Then we returned to the Bolshoi to watch the evening performance which, by good luck, was *Swan Lake*. Odette-Odile was danced by Maya Plisetskaya, who is about my own age and one of the outstanding Soviet dancers. We sat in Chulaki's box with Chaboukiani, and it was quite a family party, as Chulaki had his wife and mother and two sons with him. As I watched I thought back over my experiences of the day and decided I was not too unhappy about the prospects for Friday night, though it was obvious that not only was the choreography for Act IV completely different but also for the finales of Act II and III.

At the end, I was taken backstage and introduced to the *corps de ballet*. I was surprised when one of the swans came forward and made a speech of welcome in perfect English. It was simple and sincere and struck exactly the right note. We kissed and I felt I was becoming a part of them all.

I was also introduced to Plisetskaya and to Yuri Kondratov, who was her partner that night. I did not know then how much I was going to see of him during my tour!

15

Next we met Gennadi Rozhdestvensky, the No. 2 conductor at the Bolshoi, who had just conducted so brilliantly. In private life he is married to the young and superbly promising ballerina, Timofeyeva. With him was Asaf Messerer, ballet-master and choreographer of the new Act IV, who was to be of such great importance to me during my stay in Russia.

I had my first experience of Russian fans when I left the theatre. They crowded round me at the stage-doors, and I had to spend a long time signing autographs. Afterwards, a charming gesture, they gave me in return a book showing Plisetskaya dancing *Swan Lake*. They accompanied me all the way back to the hotel, chattering in broken English, while I tried to answer them in my broken Russian!

Monday was a lot of very hard work. I started on solos and the first mime scene; then Semeyonova showed me the second entrance and we went on to the two *pas de deux*. It was difficult in places to co-ordinate the timing—the conductor's was sometimes quite different—but I felt I was making progress. I was being watched all the time, and it was encouraging to be applauded after my Act II solo and again after the *fouettés*. I tried the Act III solo and then Messerer came and showed us the finale of Act III.

It was now well into the afternoon. We changed into fresh practice clothes and drank tea. I found my toes were very sore. But our next task was to learn the entrance in Act III, before Messerer took us all through Act IV. We went through it in great detail, and later he helped me to write it down. He was very sympathetic and I liked working with him.

We got back to the hotel by 6.30 p.m. and almost at once were invaded by two journalists from the *Moscow News*, an English-language newspaper published in Russia. One of them was a dear old man who looked as if he had come straight out of the pages of *Tolstoi*. They were photographing me when Sven started photographing them. They looked very surprised!

It had been a gruelling day, but things had gone well, and I dropped off to sleep as soon as I went to bed. I doubt if I should have slept as well if I had known what was going to happen on Tuesday.

Chapter III

## *THE CURTAIN CALLS*

THE first hint of trouble came when I arrived at the theatre the following morning. Chulaki hurried Sven away as soon as we got there. I noticed that his face showed signs of worry. So did Sven's when he returned. They told me, just as I was going on stage, that Chaboukiani had hurt his knee practising and I was to have a new partner.

The news seemed disastrous. Chaboukiani and I appeared to be dancing so well together. The initial difficulties seemed over. Now all the long hours of practice appeared to be wasted, and I should have to start once again getting accustomed to somebody else.

But there was nothing to be done. Chaboukiani had had similar trouble with his knee before. It was impossible for him to dance in three days' time and I had to make the best of it.

I hardly had time to take all this in before I was on stage. I just managed to ask who was my new partner and was slightly relieved when I was told he would be Yuri Kondratov, a pupil of Semeyonova.

He had "her" ways of working, and those, I knew, were very near to mine. And there was no question about his abilities. He was a dancer of international reputation, had partnered the great Ulanova, and was the man I had seen dancing with Plisetskaya on Sunday night. So I knew something about him.

But, still, he was a stranger. I had exchanged only a few words with him in the past. Now here was a vital rehearsal and I was appearing with him before some of the most knowledgeable people in the world of ballet. The curtains were up, the footlights were on, and I was very conscious of the spectators sitting out there in front in the darkened theatre. It was a ballerina's nightmare.

Yet everything went much better than I could possibly have expected. As happened so often on this trip, the bad things were often followed immediately by the good. And the loss of Chaboukiani was followed by the realisation that in Kondratov I had a partner of immense sympathy.

He was taller than I had thought—a good thing from my point of view—and from our very first steps together I realised that he possessed the wonderful gift of adaptability. We worked together fast and well. I kept on telling myself how lucky I was that I had been with Semeyonova for those few days and that now I was dancing with someone who shared her ideas as well. There was another thing. I was aware throughout the rehearsal of an almost palpable sympathy coming from the unofficial audience, which included Ulanova and her husband, also Plisetskaya and Yuri Zdhanov. I got the same feeling from the Bolshoi workers backstage. They realised what a blow it was for me to lose Chaboukiani at such a point, and they seemed to be willing me to do well.

We went through the entire ballet. It was a heavy strain—one of the worst in my career. Certainly I had never taken part in such a semi-public rehearsal in such trying conditions. But after two hours on the stage, rehearsing all three acts, I was amazed. Everything had gone much better than I had expected. Probably the fact that I had not had time to worry about the news had helped. Time was now very short before my opening performance, but I hoped I would be ready.

At the end of the rehearsal we sat on the side of the stage and finished writing out Act IV. Then I had a really hot shower at the theatre—such a treat after my experiences with my hotel bath—and went home to a light snack.

We had a memorable evening. Chulaki collected Sven and me at the hotel and drove us to his flat for dinner. It was quite a party. There were his wife, two sons and daughter-in-law, with Kondratov, Semeyonova, Plisetskaya, and Nicolai Fadeyechev. Completing the party were Faier, Alexander Tomski, the artistic director, and Mr Shaskin, another of the Bolshoi chiefs, who was still talking about the wonderful meals he had eaten at the pubs near Covent Garden.

This was my first experience of Russian hospitality in the home, and it was almost overwhelming. There were two enormous meal sessions. First came cold food, including a special selection of Georgian dishes for my benefit, in order to prepare me for my visit to Tiflis. I remember particularly chicken served in walnut sauce, and some exotic fish dishes.

Then we had a session of gramophone records, mostly Russian operatic music, before returning to the table for the hot dishes. Chulaki, formerly a concert pianist, played the piano, and I was convinced the eating must be over, but no: Madame Chulaki now produced a great assortment of sweetmeats, tartlets, and fruit, with coffee and chocolate. Naturally there were vodka and wines and brandy as well, and I was sorry that I could only take token sips as Chulaki kept getting up and making wonderful speeches and giving toast after toast. It was a real family party to which I felt I belonged. I was delighted with the whole atmosphere, which was warm and open-hearted, and with no gossip or backchat about other dancers. Chulaki gave us an exquisite dark-green malachite box, and then took from his own table an elegant pedestal cup and saucer and thrust them into my hands.

Outside it was snowing very hard, and Chulaki wanted to take us on a snow-drive through Moscow in his car. But I was tired, and I knew that Wednesday would be another hard day, so I went back to our hotel while Sven and other members of the party drove round the snow-covered city and saw, among other points of interest, Chaliapin's old house.

I spent most of Wednesday morning in bed before getting up for a meal which was not quite breakfast and yet was hardly a full-scale lunch. This "brunch" became a habit of ours for most of the trip. We were invited to see the noon performance of *The Sleeping Beauty* and were thrilled by Struchkova's brilliant dancing.

We rehearsed in the evening, but I felt rather tired. We only took the two *pas de deux*, and left out the solos as Semeyonova, Messerer, and Kondratov had formed a triple alliance to look after me and were very insistent that I should conserve my strength. I myself was convinced that my tiredness was only a reaction from all the nervous tension, and when I went to bed that night I certainly felt that I should be longing to dance again as soon as I got up.

But I got up sooner than I had expected. During the night I had wave after wave of nausea and soon I was very sick. This was a tragedy, for the final rehearsal was only a few hours away.

I was very ill the next morning, but I insisted on going to the theatre. I kept on telling myself that once I was on the stage and dancing I would feel better. But I crawled rather than walked across Sverdlov Square, and when I got to the Bolshoi I felt too wretched to do much warming up.

On stage I was introduced first to the company and then to the orchestra. There were little speeches and applause. I tried to acknowledge them but only managed to feel fainter in the process.

As the rehearsal was for me, most of the *corps de ballet* pieces were left out, with the result that Act II, my first act, was practically non-stop. I do not know how my dancing appeared, but at the end of the act I felt terribly sick again. My hands and face seemed to be vibrating, and I also felt curiously numb. I was helped to the dressing-rrom, and there it was obvious that I could not continue.

Dozens of people crowded to my door, and I remember Ulanova, who had been in front, appearing suddenly and being very kind. She came in, held my hand and sat with me for ten minutes, telling me not to worry about going on for the Friday performance, as another would be arranged for me.

Then a doctor and a nurse came in. I found out later they were attached permanently to the Bolshoi organisation. They got a car and had me driven the short distance from the theatre to the hotel. There they gave me tablets to swallow and a hot-water bottle to clutch, and I went to bed. Everybody kept telling me not to worry, but, of course, that was easier said than done. Here I was, about to dance at the Bolshoi, and it looked as if I shouldn't be able to leave my bed at the time when I was due to be on stage giving what I had hoped would be the performance of my life.

But this disaster illustrated a big difference between the Russians and ourselves. I had been brought up in the tradition of "the show must go on". To miss a performance for which people had bought tickets seemed to be almost a disgrace. But in the Soviet Union the attitude was quite different. First Ulanova and then other ballet people, administrators as well as dancers, assured me that there must be no question of my going on unless I was one hundred per cent fit. This was not just out of sympathy for me; I think their feeling stemmed from the idea that the performance must be staged in conditions as near perfection as possible. I noticed this

12 & 13. My first entrance in *Swan Lake* at the Bolshoi.

14. With Kondratov in Act II, *Swan Lake*.

again in the length of intervals, in the amount of work done backstage. The show was the thing; perfection was the ideal; and everything else, audience included, was subordinated. And, to give audiences their due, I think that attitude was fairly generally appreciated.

Certainly my illness meant that I should not appear on the Friday. I might be ninety-five per cent fit by then—actually I wasn't—but they didn't want a performance which was five per cent below normal. While I lay in my bed, and almost without consulting me, it was decided that I should not dance until the Sunday night—when my second performance was due—and only then if I was absolutely recovered.

. The doctor came in twice on Thursday and several times again on the following day. I had stopped being sick by then, but I was still very weak. My first sign of recovery came when I felt faintly hungry on the Friday morning. This was where the all-enveloping Bolshoi organisation came in. They decided I must have eaten something at the hotel which had disagreed with me, so for the rest of my stay in Moscow they insisted that all the food I ate must be specially prepared in their kitchens.

So at meal-times there were curious little processions across Sverdlov Square as my food was carried to my suite in huge vacuum-containers. The doctor prescribed steamed chicken and rice, porridge and fruit *compote*—and very deliciously cooked they all were.

. With the first signs of return to health came good news. Mr Mikhailov, the Minister of Culture, himself rang to ask how I was and to say that we were going to Leningrad after all, with the Tiflis visit also included. This, of course, cheered me up tremendously.

Then I heard that Ulanova had offered to give up her performance of *Giselle* at the Bolshoi the following Wednesday so that I could dance my postponed *Swan Lake* instead. What a generous and charming gesture! However, I was offered the alternative of extending my tour by a few days and coming back to dance *Swan Lake* in Moscow at the very end, and this seemed to me the better arrangement.

On Saturday I felt strong enough to get up very carefully and go to the Bolshoi again. I rehearsed there with Semeyonova,

21

Messerer, and Kondratov—I called them "my dear three" to myself—watching over me the whole time. I felt greatly relieved that my strength had returned with the rehearsal and, feeling none the worse, went back to have an early night.

All three had given me the same advice: "Sleep calmly, do not worry, and wake up feeling that you cannot wait to go on stage and dance your best." I tried hard to do this.

On Sunday I did my bar in my dressing-room, but for most of the day I rested, following the Russian example. There is no last-minute rehearsal for them. They believe that if you are not ready by the day, a few extra hours' work won't make any difference to your performance, and it is far better to spend the time relaxing.

Although it wasn't snowing it was freezing hard by the evening. There were loudspeakers in the square playing gay Russian music as we left our hotel. Sven and I almost skated across to the theatre. I had followed my advisers; I was feeling happy; and I could hardly wait to get on to the Bolshoi stage.

Semeyonova was in my dressing-room before I went on. She gave me a beautiful blue porcelain vase from her own home as a souvenir of the evening. It is near me now as I write. And I remember basket after basket of flowers from everybody, including the British Ambassador, and Ulanova.

But though I tried to keep calm, I was excited, and even the rustling of paper worried me as the performance approached. However, I was sufficiently calm to note that I had no heart-pounding—an inevitable sign of nerves before big performances in the past. Now I was just conscious of tension allied with determination. I prayed things would be all right.

Then I was on. Semeyonova and the stage-prompter mothered me from the outset, putting me on at every entrance and encouraging me as I returned to the wings. I was conscious of a great deal of sympathy and love from people I had not known eight days before. I felt I must do well.

Throughout the act I kept telling myself I must use my arms beautifully and keep my back strong and arched like the Russians. It was a strain, particularly as on so large a stage I had to cover so much ground. I also found that my shoes were too soft and I knew I must change them before the next act. The music of the large orchestra was a great inspiration, but most of all I appreciated

22

Kondratov's superb partnering. All our double work went smoothly.

At the end of the act I was very tired, and as I looked back on it I felt that I could have given more if I had not still been weak. But everybody else seemed satisfied, and I drew strength from their encouragement.

I was happier about Act III. I felt I was dancing this act better than I had ever done before, and hoped it made up for any short-comings in Act II. In the earlier act, I had been conscious of, and even slightly put off by, the whirr of cameras—the ballet was being filmed and broadcast by Moscow television—but in Act III either these had been shifted or I was too absorbed to notice them. I felt truly inspired. It was like living in another world.

There were again many curtain calls at the end of this act and then, as I was about to go to my dressing-room, I was halted by the whole company staying on stage and clapping me. Then they gave me two souvenirs—a beautifully worked horn decorated with ivory swans and a lovely hand-painted box. I remember crying a little with emotion and relief in my dressing-room.

There was a very long interval between the third and fourth acts. Then I was dancing that difficult last act with the different choreography; and then in a flash it was over. I was taking curtain-calls—to the front, to the left, to the right. There were more flowers. The end had almost a dream-like quality. I had wanted for so long to dance at the Bolshoi. There had been many hitches before it became a fact. And now it was all behind me. I might dance at the Bolshoi again, but there could never be another first time. I wept, just a little, once more.

On stage afterwards and in the Green Room, with the British, American, and Russian correspondents, and photographers crowding around, I wondered again if it had really happened. Then there was a delicious hot shower, and I was whisked off to the British Embassy in Chulaki's car.

It was not only my first performance which had been postponed from Friday but also the party given in my honour at the British Embassy. Sir Patrick and his wife, not at all put out, had switched all their arrangements. We had a wonderful dinner together, and I remember the red candles and the Christmas decorations which had just been put up in the Embassy. All the Russians who had been invited came—which, I gather, is rather unusual in Moscow. Ulanova, Plisetskaya, and my "dear three"—they were all there, all beautifully dressed. There were many Western ambassadors present, with Mr Boni and others from the Ministry of Culture, so that altogether nearly fifty of us sat down to dinner in the light of red candles which lit up beautifully the splendid Embassy glass. All the tension of the last few days gradually ebbed away in the pleasantest possible atmosphere and surroundings.

And then we drove back through the white streets, still covered with ice. The night of glory was over.

Chapter IV

## *TOAST, TU-TU'S, AND TOURING*

SUNDAY, despite the tension, had a sort of order about it,
leading up to the Bolshoi performance. Monday, in contrast,
was chaotic.

I slept only fitfully and got up early in the hope of packing before
breakfast so that there would be no desperate rush to the plane
for Kiev. But the phone kept ringing, and in between calls I
tried to write an article about my first week at the Bolshoi
which I had promised to send to the London *Sunday Times* before
Christmas.

All the time we were worrying because there was no sign of
Jhana. That meant that we had to go to the theatre by ourselves
to pack my things there. Monday is the day theatres shut in
Russia and the Bolshoi was almost deserted, the "stage-door" had
not been informed I was coming, and there was quite a delay
before we could get inside. When we managed to enter my dressing-room we had two people trying to get interviews with me for
Press and Radio. Then just when we were getting desperate about
finding somebody who would understand my luggage problems,
Yuri Kondratov arrived. He introduced some order, but even
when we got back to the hotel there were still more interviews, and
at one time I was speaking to a tape-recorder for Moscow Radio
in the hotel corridor, with the floor supervisor acting as impromptu
translator.

By 1.30 Mrs Chulaki had arrived with a car, and Yuri was also
with us, but still there was no Jhana. Fifteen minutes later she
appeared and said she had been waiting for tickets, and that we
must rush to the airport as the plane would soon take off. We
skidded rather than drove along the icy roads, but when we got to

25

the airfield we still had another thirty minutes before the aircraft was ready.

However, we had a good flight in an Ilyushin—rather like the American Convair—and at Kiev we were met by the director of the theatre, V. P. Gontar, two ballerinas in beautiful fur coats, and the two leading male dancers. They presented me with a bouquet of white chrysanthemums and azaleas. Yuri rushed to the theatre to talk with the conductor and prepare the *corps de ballet* for alterations—we planned to follow the Moscow version of *Swan Lake* as closely as possible—while the rest of us went to our hotel. I wallowed in a hot bath—the first hot water since England, except for the Bolshoi showers—and by 9 p.m. was in bed.

Next morning I was up early for rehearsal on stage with the full company and orchestra. It was a lovely theatre but the stage seemed small after the Bolshoi—it was about the same size as Covent Garden's—and had a rather tricky rake. The girls generally seemed taller than at the Bolshoi. The orchestra maintained a good tempo because Boris Chistiakov the conductor picked up immediately what I wanted. I found later that he was an ex-dancer, which undoubtedly helped. Yuri had made arrangements so well the previous night that there were only a few alterations to make, except in Act IV which was again quite different. At the end there was a lot of applause and handshaking and hugging.

We did not get back to the hotel until late afternoon. After the long wide corridors and caverns of the Metropole I thought it charming. It was smaller and more countrified, and its lace curtains and pretty porcelain gave it a Victorian air in contrast to the Edwardian plushiness of Moscow. Our room looked on to the tree-lined main street with trams passing every few minutes, but we had double windows which kept out the noise for most of the visit.

On Wednesday I spent as much time as possible resting, for that night was my second performance of *Swan Lake* in Russia. On what was to have been my first night in Moscow I had been ill; now, by coincidence, it was poor Sven's turn. He, too, had tummy trouble, but he managed to get over the worst of it in a day.

The performance went well. I felt very happy, apart from the nervous excitement one always experiences; the tremendous strain of my first performance in Russia was over. I got a good reception from the audience after each act, but equally gratifying was the response of the company who lined the corridors and applauded each time I went to my dressing-room. Yuri partnered superbly. We were really getting to know each other by this time. I was specially moved when at the end of Act III the company presented me with some Ukrainian dancers in porcelain—"to remind you of your visit to the Kiev ballet"—and the leading ballerina gave me a white practice slip in a material resembling nylon, which she herself had made for me.

It was all very friendly and I went home with a great feeling of relief. Looking back now, the late supper I had in celebration appears rather curious; semolina porridge and baked apples. But it was just what I wanted at the time.

The following day we got up late—Sven was almost well again—and I went to the theatre and rehearsed *Giselle* for two hours. We worked hard and I was very thrilled with the new lifts. In the evening we heard the American singer, Blanche Thébom, in *Carmen*. She sang and acted with verve and authority, but I was interested to see that she also had difficulties in her strange surroundings. On one occasion she picked up a flower-pot but found it mounted on a board to which were attached several others!

We sat in the director's box and at the intervals went into another of his rooms and were offered wine and the mineral water—a pleasanter version of Vichy—which the Russians drink in incredible quantities. After the opera we had dinner in our room with Yuri and Jhana. There was a long discussion about ballet, which was a stimulating end to one of the pleasantest days we had had so far.

On Friday I gave my second performance in Kiev—again *Swan Lake*. This time things went even better. Yuri's partnering was a joy and an inspiration. I was also impressed with the company. They had wonderful backs, excellent elevation and high extensions; but I was inclined to think they were more athletic than the Bolshoi dancers, with less lyricism and poetry. After the performance the theatre director came in with a big smile and gave me another wonderful present—a pair of Ukrainian boots specially made for me in red leather. He was very proud that they had got the exact size.

27

As usual, on the day after a performance I stayed in bed as late as possible, while Sven went out with Yuri and Jhana to buy an icon. I rehearsed *Giselle* all afternoon, and we had a quiet evening in our hotel room.

On Sunday I danced *Swan Lake* again and, with Yuri and I now in closer harmony, this performance once more brought improvements. This, indeed, was an idyllic time. I was dancing as well as I have ever done, I was receiving absolute co-operation from my partner and the company, and conditions in Kiev were very good.

The hotel was quiet, full of little old men in beards, and at times it gave me an impression that I was living in a sort of Cheltenham-on-Dnieper! There was an enthusiastic ballet public at Kiev, which of course was a great joy. Crowds followed us every time we left the theatre. It was here that I experienced one gesture that I shall always remember. As I came out once I found the usual crowd round the stage-door, but I noticed a man with two loaves of bread. More to make conversation than anything else, I said in halting Russian: "Those loaves look good." "Take them, really they are good," he said instantly. I got the feeling that so intense was their love and respect for the ballet that he would have given me anything he possessed. I could not refuse the bread in view of the way in which it was offered, so I took it back to the hotel and we had it with supper. But my idle words turned out to be very true. It was not only good bread; it was the best we had throughout our trip and, indeed, some of the best I have ever eaten.

Kiev was now in the midst of Independence celebrations, the fortieth anniversary of the Bolshevik victory in the Ukraine. Mr Krushchev was in town and everywhere there were red flags, red stars, and huge pictures of Lenin. But there were no pictures of the contemporary Soviet leaders except when they appeared in groups showing the Praesidium (which I suppose is roughly comparable with our Cabinet).

The main effect of the Independence celebrations on us was to keep us awake. There were loudspeakers everywhere relaying music, speeches, and songs, and in the streets there was almost continual commotion. Even our double windows were not proof against this.

28

15. With Kondratov in Act III, *Swan Lake*.

16

17

18

16, 17 & 18. Act III, *Swan Lake*, at Kiev.

19. At the end of the Coda in Act III, *Swan Lake*, at the Bolshoi.

20. Taking a curtain call after Act III, *Swan Lake*, at the Bolshoi.

We should have flown to Tiflis that day, but there turned out to be no plane. We never could find out exactly what went wrong, but gathered it was something to do with winter schedules! There was the alternative of leaving at midnight or flying on Tuesday, and we chose the latter. So we spent Monday sightseeing but the weather was disappointing. The snow was melting, there was a mist everywhere, and altogether it was not unlike a rather nasty thaw in London. There were Christmas trees in all the streets and in many windows in preparation for the big Russian winter holiday, which comes on New Year's Day. But the shops were poorly dressed, and Sven had a trying time attempting unsuccessfully to buy a map of Russia and some large envelopes.

I managed to visit two churches there, both containing richly decorated icons and innumerable murals. At one, a Russian Orthodox service was in progress. It was full of people—mostly over the age of about forty, I thought—though I was interested to see several young priests officiating. The other one I visited was the famous Cathedral of St Sophia, built some time in the eleventh century. I had been intrigued by a distant glimpse of its gleaming golden domes and wanted to have a closer look. Apparently this cathedral, formerly connected by a tunnel with the Prince's Palace, was being restored as a museum, and much work was going on there. On many walls several layers of paintings, from different periods, were being uncovered. I liked very much the frescoes of eleventh-century court life which included curious circus-like scenes, as though a Byzantine Dame Laura Knight had been at work there.

The next day could not have been less like Christmas Eve. I felt a little homesick. We were up at 5.45, ready to go to the plane, but we were kept hanging about until the early afternoon, and were then told that we should not be flying at all that day owing to the weather. This was puzzling, as there seemed to be no fog. However, I decided that we must send a telegram announcing that if we couldn't fly that day I couldn't dance in Tiflis the next evening. That seemed quite reasonable, as it would be impossible for me to dance at anything approaching my best after a ten-hours' flight. Jhana could not be made to see this, and we had quite a struggle before we persuaded her to send the telegram.

We felt very gloomy as the day ebbed away, but then Yuri came in and we all had tea in our room, and suddenly it didn't seem such a bad sort of Christmas Eve after all. The four of us talked away and actually started to dance. Soon Yuri and I were busy practising *Giselle* in the hotel room, and so time flew by.

Christmas Day started with another early call, but after an hour Jhana rang to say the airport was still closed down, so Sven and I just lay on our beds, fully clothed, and went back to sleep. We slept for more than an hour before we were awakened by a panic call from Jhana, saying, "Come at once." We made a dash by car to the airport and got there at 10.15, but had to wait in an office for nearly an hour before we were allowed into the plane.

The Kiev company, considerate as ever, had a representative waiting there to bid us good-bye. He gave me a rather wilted bouquet and revealed he had been there with it since the previous morning. Several other members of the company had been out from time to time, but they could not get news of our revised flight arrangements.

This time our Ilyushin was not so good. The springs in the seats had gone, the safety straps did not work; it was all rather below B.E.A. standards! There were as usual no refreshments on board, but we stopped at Dnepropetrovsk and Stalingrad and I managed to get tea each time. I noticed that the other passengers often brought sandwiches, oranges, and chocolate with them, as we used to on our war-time journeys. At Stalingrad the other three tried dark *kasha*—something like brown bird-seed!—with meat and onions on top, but they were hardier than I, for I could only tackle dry toast that day. As we flew low over Stalingrad I could not help marvelling at the reconstruction of this brave city whose name symbolised the whole of the Russian resistance to Hitlerism.

We got to Rostov about 4 p.m.—in London it would have been 7 p.m., and Ingvar's Christmas Day would have been over. All the time Sven and I had been thinking of him, and we were glad we had at least got each other on this strangest of all Christmas Days.

We were just leaving the plane when there was a loudspeaker announcement. This seemed to electrify Jhana and she rushed off. Yuri explained the plane for Tiflis was taking off in ten minutes and she had gone for tickets. But soon afterwards she rushed back and said it would not be taking off at all that day. So we were

30

condemned to spend Christmas night in the transit hotel at the airport!

This was in a wing leading off the main airport building. The rooms were clean and modern, with light-wood furniture which was a pleasant relief after the heaviness at our two previous hotels. We also saw the first domestic pet I had noticed since entering Russia. This was a lovely white cat, who soon seemed quite devoted to us and purred herself into a frenzy as she wrapped herself round our legs.

There was no water in the bathroom; the bulbs were giving out hardly any light; and the radio in our room didn't work. It didn't seem a very pleasant prospect. So far the pleasantest thing about Christmas Day had been the little chocolate bears which Yuri and Jhana had given us as unexpected presents when we met in the morning.

Feeling rather depressed, we went into the hotel dining-room. There was one long table where somebody had been giving a wonderful party. The debris of what had obviously been a memorable but hastily terminated meal was still there. Although it did not feel like Christmas Day, Yuri and Jhana were determined to give us a little celebration. They insisted on ordering champagne which, when it came, was a strange dark red colour.

Soon we had all cheered up. We found a piano and, with Yuri playing, we sang and danced and told each other that it wasn't such a bad Christmas after all. But by eight o'clock I was dozing off. After a cup of tea I was glad to go to sleep and forget about the disappointment of having to miss what should have been my first performance in Tiflis. I only hoped Intourist were keeping the theatre informed about our progress.

Sure enough, we were roused again at 5.45. We had breakfast all together, but I couldn't face the cheese and salami with garlic the others ate, so I had toast and marmalade. After the previous day's experience I took plenty of hard dry toast with me, and felt prepared for anything.

But things went better today. We took off as dawn was breaking over the frozen ground and when the sun came up we were high over the Caucasian mountains. This was breath-taking, and Sven could not resist grabbing his cine-camera to take this awe-inspiring sight. Unfortunately the noise of our twenty-five-year-old camera

31

must have attracted the air-hostess, for she rushed up and forbade Sven to take any more. We were to hear more about this later!

Our plane seemed a friendly sort of machine, filled mainly with peasants. There were strings of onions and other vegetables rolling about the luggage compartment where normally one would expect to find hide suitcases.

Getting out at Tiflis airport the air was crisp and fresh, and we rejoiced to find the sun warm on our faces. But as soon as we got into the airport building my heart sank, for a uniformed official led Sven away. The next quarter of an hour was one of the longest I had ever known. At last Sven came back and, to my relief, he seemed none the worse. He explained that he had been interrogated by six officials who had told him that by international law he was forbidden to film from the air. He apologised and, as requested, left the film for them to develop. However, he forgot to say he had been taking colour. So a few days later another man came to see us and confessed with much apology that all the film had been ruined.

Soon a car arrived with a charming Intourist man and we drove towards Tiflis. In some ways the country was reminiscent of Chile—flat and sandy, with snow-covered mountains in the distance. On the way we met another car which stopped, and out tumbled three of the theatre directors. They had known nothing about our whereabouts until they learned our plane had arrived. After tremendous apologies from them we went on to our hotel.

The rooms were good, with high ceilings, and our only complaint was of an all-pervading smell of disinfectant every time we went into a corridor. But the food was good—not too spicy, as we had been told it would be in Georgia—and we were touched to see that they had found a tiny Union Jack to put on our table in the restaurant together with a Russian flag.

We went straight to the theatre to rehearse from three until five. The stage had a better surface than at Kiev and was not so raked. There was almost an atmosphere of a performance during our rehearsal. There were watchers everywhere—in the wings, in front, and positively leaning out of the boxes. Chaboukiani welcomed us and said that he had wired Moscow to see if he could partner me in this, his own theatre, but we had already left when his telegram arrived. I was touched by his suggestion. I soon found that in Georgia he is a national hero, and his dancing has made him as famous in that part of the world as, say, Stanley Matthews is in England.

After a quick bath and thirty minutes' rest at the hotel, we dashed back to the theatre to see Chaboukiani's ballet *Othello*. This was only its second performance. On our way to and from our box during the intervals the crowds lined the corridors to let us pass. It was like being a princess. From the stage Chaboukiani introduced us to the audience. It was a wonderful gesture to share one of his nights of triumph with a foreigner who had not even danced in his city.

And a night of triumph for Chaboukiani it really was. The audience showed fiery, typically Georgian enthusiasm. I understand the success has since been repeated in Moscow where the same company performed to sold-out houses. It is the type of ballet which I think appeals particularly to Soviet audiences. Full-length and highly dramatic, it has plenty of excuse for varied stage effects.

It was a faithful translation of Shakespeare into dance, mime, and music, and to me it conveyed admirably the tension of the story. The ballet had four acts—thirteen scenes in all—and lasted for four hours, including the three intervals. This, I feel, would be too long for the average Western audience. It is fair to say, however, that the interest was sustained throughout, and the public lived fully the joys, the suspicions, and the agonies of Othello and his world.

How much of this was due to Chaboukiani's choreography, and how much to his own fine performance was difficult to determine. I think the ballet would lose a tremendous amount if he were not taking the main part. As the Moor he had a superb make-up. He riveted one's attention whenever he was on the stage —which was fairly often—by the strength of his portrayal and dynamic dancing. It was obvious that he had given detailed study to the play and had steeped himself deeply in the role.

The music, written for the ballet by the Georgian composer A. Machavariani, contained romance, drama, and tragedy. It was in modern style, with many melodies and strong rhythms, lyrical in the love passages and strident in the dramatic ones. The costumes and scenery were designed by C. B. Virsaladze, who also

33

designed the present *Swan Lake* at the Bolshoi Theatre. His *décor* for *Othello* was effective and the ingenious use of black-outs and spotlights added to the impact of the story. Economy in the use of scenery showed imagination and practicality. The well-designed costumes were often of daring colours, as in the wedding feast scene, with many shades of orange and mauve on the court ladies. In this same scene there was an exciting dance by Moorish women. When Chaboukiani joined this dance he added such fire and rhythm to the bare-foot stamps that he completely stopped the performance.

There were many peasant dances throughout. The comparatively small amount of classical ballet appeared mostly in the *pas-de-deux* sequences between Othello and Desdemona, who was movingly portrayed by V. Tsignadze. M. Grishkevitch was outstanding as Emilia, and Z. Kikaleishvili made an appropriately hateful Iago.

Chaboukiani had created for a large company, and the stage often appeared too small for the pattern of the dances to be seen to maximum advantage. The battle scene was presented as a flashback on the dark, spotlighted stage and showed realistically the storming of the battlements. The audience also enjoyed the dramatic arrival of Othello in a large ship, with sails blowing in theatrical winds across the back of the stage: and the final scene with its long foreboding flights of steps, eerily lit, behind the bed where Othello murdered Desdemona.

I had wanted for many years to see *Othello* as a ballet. It was curious that I should travel to Tiflis to have this wish fulfilled. The Georgian people are specially fond of Shakespeare, and I am told it translates better into the Georgian language than perhaps any other. Certainly the reception that evening was one of the biggest I have ever seen.

Chapter V

## IN RUSSIA'S DEEP SOUTH
## AND FROZEN NORTH

OUR first full day in Tiflis was also the day of my first *Giselle* in the Soviet Union. But there was less of the tension which marked my first *Swan Lake*. I was relaxed enough to take in all the charm of this fine Georgian town as we walked to the theatre in the morning.

Although it was December 27th most of the trees still had their autumn colourings of gold and yellow. It was like finding a British St Martin's Summer. The town itself gave me an Eastern feeling, with the gay skirts of the women, the swarthy skins of the fine-looking men, and the cypresses dotting the eastern hillsides. At times there was the impression of a Persian miniature.

*Giselle* that evening was a wonderful experience for me. I had been afraid that my acting would appear pale in comparison with the Russian's, but I lost myself in the role as soon as I went to the stage. I was convinced that the first act was the best I had ever done. The mime was improved. I put that down to the fine acting of Yuri, and the influence of *Othello* and other ballets I had seen during my short stay. I felt much less restrained, and I realised that night how much I was gaining from dancing with the Russians.

Yuri was once again superb. He must be among the two or three best male dancers in the world. For me, he was certainly the perfect partner. That night brought more of those kindnesses which the Russian dancers lavish on a stranger to make him feel at home and welcome. When I came to the theatre, I found a little pot of baby narcissi in my dressing-room from the dancer who was to appear as my mother in *Giselle*, with a note saying that she had lost her heart to her "daughter". Then between the acts there were

35

photographs with the company, who left me in no doubt about their feeling of friendship for me. At the end there were masses of flowers and I remember particularly a tribute from Chaboukiani— a long, shallow basket filled with blooms, wild berries, including mistletoe, and ceramic jars. This apparently was a typically Georgian gift, as I received other similar baskets before I left.

I was so warmly received that I felt very deeply the fact that I could not give an extra performance the following night. People had refused to take back their money for the performance which I missed owing to the aeroplane hold-up and had held on to their tickets in the hope that I would also dance on the Saturday. But I was due to perform again on Sunday and fly back to Moscow on Monday. I was beginning to feel the effects of our travelling experiences, and I was fearful that full-length classics on three successive nights, followed by the long, thousand-mile trip back to Moscow, would really be too much. It would have been impossible to give good performances in such circumstances.

So while the audience cried *"Saftra, saftra"* ("Tomorrow, tomorrow") as I took my curtain calls, I was wondering all the time if I could, in fact, fit in an extra *Giselle*. The theatre authorities said that either this or *Swan Lake* would be equally acceptable. But in my heart, though I wanted so much to appear three times, I knew I should not do it, and in the end, most reluctantly, I said I couldn't. But to refuse made me very sad.

We were awakened next morning by representatives of the theatre who still hoped to persuade me to change my mind. I had to say firmly that it would not be possible and then I went back to bed for another two hours.

After a late lunch we went for a drive round Tiflis. It really was the most "foreign" place we visited. The Georgians are particularly proud of its long history, and I was repeatedly told that they are one of the oldest peoples in the world. We delighted in the narrow cobbled streets, the sudden hills, and above all the sense of colour and light and warmth. Indeed, its very name is significant, for the people call their town Tbilisi, which is derived from the Georgian word "tbili", meaning warmth. The warmth in the town's name refers to the hot springs for which it is famous. We found these springs that afternoon on a long, rocky precipice on one side of the River Kura. But there was also a modern Tiflis,

21. With Kondratov in the first *pas de deux* in Act IV, *Swan Lake*.

22. The end of the first *pas de deux* in Act IV, *Swan Lake*.

where we saw some of the best shops in Russia. We had not noticed any vegetables for sale in other parts of the Soviet Union we visited, but we saw fine displays here.

. That night I was interviewed on television—most of my spare time seemed to be taken up by interviews for either TV or radio or newspapers—and to get to the studio we were taken up a funicular railway. Carpeted below, we could see the thousand lights of Tiflis reflected in the River Kura, while at the top we found our studio in the middle of the large Stalin Park. Accommodation was cramped by British television standards. There was only one studio, and the room in which they did all the mixing was also used as the artists' waiting-room. The pictures on the screen were very clear and the quality compared quite well with our own.

Jhana, who was to do the interpreting, told us she was terrified, but we kept telling her this would make her into a film-star and her husband would be proud of her! I was interviewed sitting on a little Victorian chair, with a round table covered by a lace table-cloth in the background. I thought our interviewer looked a very severe young woman, but she soon relaxed when we got going, and it was a thoroughly agreeable quarter of an hour. It finished when I was given another of the huge wicker baskets of flowers and berries—a "Chaboukiani basket", as we called it.

We were taken home by car—the funicular had stayed open later than usual specially to take us up—and we decided to dine downstairs in the restaurant. This proved to be a happy decision, because we were at once greeted by three Georgians at the adjoining table who showed they knew who we were by toasting us. We acknowledged their toast and at once they sent over a large bottle of Soviet Benedictine as a present. Soon the whole restaurant was delightedly watching our new friends giving toast after toast, and the band joined in the fun by playing what they imagined were typical British tunes. Their selection consisted of "Auld Lang Syne"—played very slowly—"Oh Johnny", and "I'll Be Loving You Always". Jhana and Yuri sang, we were taught Georgian and Russian songs, and the meal passed in a haze of goodwill and brave attempts to understand each other's popular music. We returned to our room laden with oranges, chocolates, and more liqueurs—all gifts from our admirers.

Sunday, a performance day, was as restful as I could make it,

37

while Sven went out to try to buy a battery for his flash-equipment and an oriental carpet. He failed to get either. Shopping in the Soviet Union was usually rather unsuccessful.

But *Giselle* made up for this. It had a wonderful reception. It was televised, and my only disappointment was that all my new friends disappeared as soon as the performance was over. It was true that the director, Dimitri Mchedlidze, came into my room afterwards with a huge brown-paper parcel containing five bottles of Georgia's famous red wine and another five bottles of white, but I was getting so used to charming little speeches of welcome and farewell that now I noticed it if they were missing. I firmly told myself that I had been spoiled in the other places, and I must come down to earth again at some point. But when I got back to the hotel I found why everybody had disappeared. There had been a great conspiracy to give me a surprise party.

Everybody was there—Chaboukiani, by this time an old friend; ballerina Vera Tzignadze; the composer of *Othello*, Alexander Machavariani; the three theatre directors and the conductor D. Mirtzhulava. All these warm Georgian people seemed to have injected some of their own southern sunshine into their lives. A great table was laden with food, which included all the famous Georgian delicacies we had been told about. I remember with pleasure the exquisite hot cheese dishes. One particularly exotic titbit was pickled mimosa, and this was followed by *shashlik* on a flaming sword.

I was presented with a Georgian silver drinking horn. Everybody had to drink from it first and make a speech. But apparently this was not enough, for it is the custom there also to drink symbolically from the largest vessel in the room—and in Georgia to drink means to empty! A fruit-bowl was chosen for this ceremony, and I felt rather mean because I did not join in. Most of the men emptied this twice, but I noticed Yuri was content to do it once, explaining that he had to rehearse with me the next day.

Our flight back was simplicity itself compared with our trip to Tiflis. At the airport the director and other officials of the theatre were there to present us with bouquets and offer a little breakfast before we took off. The aeroplane was much more comfortable, but we were scheduled again to land at Rostov and three other places. Suddenly, however, I looked down and saw we were flying over water. This was very surprising, but I was told it was the Black Sea and nobody seemed worried. Then we landed at a small watering-place and wandered about for an hour, expecting more of the delays which had marked our journey to the south. But just when we were getting resigned we were ordered back to the plane, which proceeded to take off and fly smartly non-stop to Moscow, missing out all the intermediate stops. We never did discover what had caused all this change and were too thankful to pursue the matter. But I often wonder what happened to the people waiting for our plane at Rostov and the other places!

In Moscow we were taken to the Metropole. It was almost like returning home. We had gone through so much there that we had come to have quite an affection for the place. Even the cold bath water was forgiven; and now, as if to show it repaid our affection, the hotel suddenly produced piping-hot water from every tap. We had also gone up in the world, for instead of our previous quarters, we now had a luxurious four-roomed suite with a grand piano in the sitting-room.

When I went to the Bolshoi the next morning I felt more relaxed and confident than before. In the director's room I noticed a little fir tree being decorated and was given a few ornaments of the type which we use on Christmas trees in Britain. I hung these up in my dressing-room, and put out the Christmas cards we had received from home, so that we had our little feeling of celebration too.

I saw Ulanova in the rehearsal-room and at once she wanted to know all about our tour. Her opinion was that we had had a really heavy schedule. As I watched her in class I could not help admiring again her lovely feet, the swiftness of her head movement when she turned, and, above all, the incredible combination of lightness and strength.

It was good to meet Semeyonova and Faier and Messerer again. We had an inspired *Swan Lake* rehearsal, followed by the usual Radio and Press interviews. As I went back to the hotel I saw everything was closing down. It was New Year's Eve, and the Russians were getting ready for their big holiday of the winter. I did not go out that night, but Sven went to see *Eugene Onegin* at the Bolshoi.

The New Year's Day performance at the theatre was to be a gala affair, so I was naturally anxious to do well again. The

39

director made a special New Year's speech to the company before the curtain went up. I was told that it was also the eight hundredth performance of *Swan Lake* in that theatre.

This time I was better able to obey the usual advice about being restful and happy and longing to dance. It was true: I just couldn't wait to go on. I wanted particularly to show everybody how well Yuri and I were working together. I was reinforced, too, by one of the kindest actions I have ever seen in the world of ballet. Plisetskaya devoted her whole evening to being with me during the performance. She was with me in dressing-room and wings, guiding me on and off, and giving me, from her own knowledge of the Bolshoi, little suggestions as, for instance, where to start and finish, on this large stage.

There were lots of curtain calls, the audience was extremely warm, and I went home very thankful that things had gone so well. A crowd of fans followed us, and their friendliness and enthusiasm made a good end to a wonderful New Year's Day.

We had lunch at the Swedish Embassy the following afternoon, and it was quite a family party, for the Ambassador and his wife, Mr and Mrs Sohlman, had their two sons, and Sir Patrick and Lady Reilly arrived with their daughter. Mr Sohlman is the doyen of the diplomatic corps in Moscow and his Russian-born wife is a great balletomane. Sven, of course, is Swedish, so it made a happy Anglo-Swedish occasion. We were both delighted to see the Christmas decorations and a typical Swedish gingerbread house. We went shopping later in the afternoon and bought lovely porcelain figures and some beautifully painted boxes, but unfortunately Children's World, the big department store devoted entirely to children, was closed, so we could not buy any presents for Ingvar.

One pleasant surprise was a telephone call from *The Star* in London. It was exciting to hear my own language coming all the way from my home town, and we were given the reassuring news that all was going well in our home.

In the evening we had drinks with ITV producer, Michael Ingrams, who had been making a one-hour documentary on Russia, and the ITV programme controller, John McMillan. Then we dashed to the Stanislavsky Theatre for the second night of the new ballet, *Joan of Arc*. There was a long interval, and as we were leaving for Leningrad that night we could only stay for the first two acts. Behind us were some students from Sweden and one from Canada and, hearing us speak English, they spoke to us. The Canadian asked if I had seen Beryl Grey dancing the previous night and seemed thrilled with the performance. It was fun then to introduce myself!

It was hard to leave this well-dressed and imaginative production without having seen all of the ballet. But as it was impossible to stay, it means that I cannot now write of this ballet as a whole.

The Stanislavsky Nemirovitch-Dantchenko Company is smaller and younger than the Bolshoi. It has not such a high standard of dancing, but it has fresh and original ideas to give to productions of new and classical ballets.

The *Joan of Arc* ballet, with a libretto by B. V. Pletnova, was divided into three acts of seven scenes. It was beautifully designed by V. I. Rindin. Here was a designer who made a valuable contribution to the production.

I liked particularly a court scene, showing the Dauphin surrounded by his courtiers in a convincing period atmosphere, with beautiful costumes making a colourful picture against the chequered stage-cloth and stained-glass windows at the back. There was more classical ballet-dancing here than in the other scenes I saw. Up to the time we left there had been predominantly peasant dances and dramatic battle scenes, well-staged and much helped by expert lighting.

Most of the choreography was by Burmeister, but it was well known in Moscow that Ulanova had also spent many months working on it. It may have been my imagination, but I felt sure that she had arranged a lot of Joan's work. It was easy to imagine Ulanova in that role, with its exquisite little runs and *bourrées* and swift jumps—all things in which she excels. It was also possible to visualise her in the stirring moments of spiritual revelation and strength which Joan was required to portray. I know it had been hoped that Ulanova would create the role, but in the end it was V. T. Bovt who danced it. She shared the role with another ballerina, E. Vlassova.

Though slight in build, Bovt was a striking figure, particularly when she appeared in black tights and silver-mesh jerkin, which showed to perfection her beautifully shaped legs and compact body. Her small, sensitive face was well suited to this conception of Joan, as an almost frail young girl, pathetic and feminine, but still a compelling personality in the battle scenes.

I liked also the music which was by the young composer H. I. Peilo. It was with this music still ringing in our ears that we dashed to the station, where we found more fans waiting to see us off. They gave us an album of ballet pictures and—a gesture I shall always remember—a box of chocolate coins because they had heard I had a little boy back in England.

The Red Arrow, on which we went to Leningrad, is one of the prestige trains of the Soviet Union. Sven and I had a sleeping compartment with two single beds, table, and radio. Everything was clean and comfortable, and a woman attendant brought us tea the next morning. We left Moscow at 11.55 p.m. and were in Leningrad the next morning a few minutes before the scheduled time of 9.20 a.m.

We stayed in the elegant Astoria Hotel, opposite St Isaac's Cathedral, and they gave us what we christened the English Suite. It consisted of an enormous bedroom, a lavish drawing-room, a dining-room, a writing-room, two bathrooms—and a genuine English silver tea-service, complete with the addition of samovar. This was the only one we saw in Russia.

We found that we had not been expected until Saturday, and were billed to dance *Swan Lake*, not *Giselle*, but that was soon altered. We went to look at Leningrad. At the old Winter Palace we spent three hours seeing the famous Hermitage collection of paintings. This must be one of the finest in the world. There were huge crowds there of all ages, and we were struck again by the popularity of the arts in the Soviet Union.

Leningrad as a city impressed us very much. It is beautifully laid out with many wide streets, numerous canals, and countless bridges. Every time we went out we felt surrounded by the ghosts of the past.

In the evening we saw the visiting French ballerina, Liane Daydé, dance *Giselle*, partnered by her fellow-countryman, Michel Renault. The renowned Leningrad Company danced sensitively, but, I thought, did not use their arms and backs as well as the Bolshoi. I was impressed by the beauty of the theatre: a perfect blend of blue, white, and gold, as perfect in its distinctive way as the red and gold of the Bolshoi. It is now called the Kirov, but it used to be known, of course, as the Maryinsky.

On Saturday we went right through *Giselle* but it took a long time. I was not so clear about their mime scenes. I was better prepared, however, for the stage-effects from my previous experience of *Giselle* in Tiflis.

The following day was to be my last performance in Russia. By now my husband and I were both anxious to get home as fast as possible, but we were also sad that our trip was ending. Sven, who had been trying to buy caviare the previous day, had failed to find any, but he was saved by the hotel producing eight small jars. It would have been impossible to have returned from Russia without caviare!

Yuri and I were very well received for our last *Giselle* together. The lifts with him were most comfortable and I have never enjoyed a *Giselle* more. There were speeches on stage afterwards, but I was rather perturbed not to have seen much of Jhana during the early evening. She had mysteriously disappeared after presenting me with a beautiful "dying Swan" statue of Ulanova. But when we got to the train all was explained. She had been busy making preparations for a surprise party which she was giving us with Yuri.

So, as the Red Arrow left the station, out came caviare, chicken, cheese, chocolate, tangerines, bread and butter, wine, vodka, and tea. The train attendants entered into the spirit of the thing and produced glasses, napkins, and cutlery. Jhana had even got special currant cakes which she said would remind us of home. "Just like English cakes, yes?" she said. (Actually, no!)

It was a wonderful finale to the trip. The four of us—Yuri and Jhana, Sven and I—had been together so much, we had known triumph together and occasionally a few feelings of despair. We represented three nations but had become firm friends. It was one of the happiest nights of my life as we sat and talked, and were conscious all the time of the genuine affection in which we held each other.

In Moscow an Embassy car swept us off to breakfast with Lady Reilly and then we were back at the Metropole. A quick trip to the Kremlin—oh, how many things we wanted to do but there was no time!—and then we were driving once more to the airport. But this time we were going home.

43

Chulaki was ill but his wife came with us, and so did Tomski and many other people we had grown to know as friends. Dear Jhana was in tears at the end, and Yuri, who had brought his wife, was for once almost silent. He had cracked so many jokes during the tour, but now he had little to say. Sven and I too felt the same. I wanted to go home, but I would have liked so much to have taken many of those dear people at the airport with us. But the aeroplane would not wait, and soon our TU104 was climbing high above the airport, above the Bolshoi and the Metropole and the British Embassy and all the other places where we had left a little of our hearts. I chewed bread hopefully as a precaution against ear trouble, and tried to realise that my trip was over.

23. As Odette in her first sorrowful dance, Act IV, *Swan Lake*.

24. The swan-maidens gather round the broken-hearted Odette.

25. The swan-maidens grouped round Odette, protecting her from the Magician.

26. With Kondratov in Act IV, *Swan Lake*, at the Bolshoi.

*PART TWO*

# The Soviet Ballet

Chapter VI

## THE GREAT THEATRE

BOLSHOI in Russian means great, and the Bolshoi Theatre was named for its size. It could not have a better name. It is a theatre which is great in every sense. The scale on which it operates, the lavishness of its resources and, indeed, its whole approach make it something unique in the world of ballet and opera.

It employs about 2,800 people, or almost the population of a small township. It seats 2,200, while the smaller theatre attached to it—called the Bolshoi *filiale*—seats another 1,900. The ballet company itself numbers more than 220, while the reserve is 300 Bolshoi pupils. The stage measures 85 feet wide and is 185 feet deep. About 77 feet of this depth is used for performances of ballet. There are 200 musicians, about half of whom usually take part at a ballet performance.

These statistics are impressive in themselves and indicate, I think, the importance which the Soviet authorities attach to ballet. Only an artistic organisation backed by the State to a considerable degree could have such resources. But the figures by themselves go only a small way towards providing an impression of the spirit which I found throughout the Bolshoi.

There was a feeling of complete dedication which I have met nowhere else. Mainly, this came from the members of the organisation who were doing something so superlatively well that it marked them out from the rest of the ballet world. Part of the feeling stemmed, too, from tradition; and another part from the realisation that in their country they were regarded as people making a special contribution to society.

This last factor was naturally one of the things which struck me

47

most when I looked at the Bolshoi as a dancer interested in the standards of her profession. It was intriguing to notice that comfort did not stop at the pass-door. There were carpets and other amenities behind stage as well as in the front of the house.

Indeed, by Western theatre standards a Russian dancer is almost pampered. The backstage staff seemed to me immense. I had, of

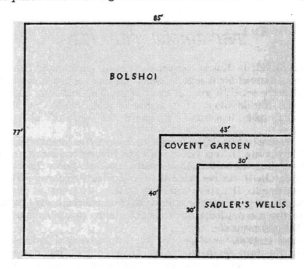

course, a dresser, as in Britain. But there was also a dresser for hair, a dresser for make-up, and another dresser to wet-white the body.

The make-up was provided by the theatre, and was changed at every interval if necessary. There were even special women just to take dancers to and from the showers, and always I found a woman waiting to wash my back!

Another woman brought tea with lemon at the intervals and somebody was constantly changing towels in the dressing-rooms and bringing fresh soap. There were, in fact, women everywhere, even shifting the props. That was one thing which still appeared strange to me right up to the end of my stay.

48

In my dressing-room there was an air of spaciousness which not even the considerable amount of furniture could eliminate. I had a bar along one side and was able to practise here as much as I wanted. The room had two easy chairs, three upright chairs and a settee, as well as the dressing-table and a smaller table on which was a constantly replenished jug of water. If I wanted food there was a canteen on the premises which was always open during the day and until the end of the performance. On the walls there were pictures of famous ballerinas and singers of the past and present. The whole provided a feeling of comfort and cosiness. The radio in each dressing-room gave ordinary programmes when it was not relaying from the stage.

There was a large mirror just before one went on stage, and near by was a comfortable room with large mirrors and red velvet-covered seats along the walls. There was a similar "green room" to the left of the stage where I was interviewed and photographed after that memorable first performance.

Attached to the theatre was a clinic with full-time doctor, dentist, nurses, physiotherapists, and masseurs. There was even a weekly newspaper written entirely by the Bolshoi Company. One really did get the impression of being in a small, but separate, town.

The theatre has three large classrooms and, in each, three one-hour classes are given every day. The Bolshoi Company has five resident teachers: Yekaterina Gerdt, Asaf and Sulamith Messerer, Petrova, and Semeyonova. A dancer chooses to study under the one with whom he is most in sympathy. The Bolshoi School pupils also have the benefit of these great teachers for the last few years of their training.

In addition to these classes—which are conducted from 10 a.m. to 1 p.m.—it was obvious that the dancers who wish to reach the front rank also did a considerable amount of work on their own, as one would expect. I was told, however, that there were few private lessons.

The rehearsal-room in which I worked was very large, raked like the stage, with bars round three sides and a mirror running along the fourth. There were plenty of windows, so it was always very light and, thank goodness, it was well heated, as was the entire theatre. After classes these three rooms were free for rehearsals, but the stage could also be made available from 9.30 a.m. onwards for rehearsals of new productions and revivals.

49

All costumes and shoes were made on the premises. I was impressed with the design of the costumes. Sometimes Western dancers are weighed down by heavy materials. In Russia the majority of the costumes seemed very light and flowed beautifully, without hindering movement and without showing the line of the body. The tu-tu's were made of cotton tarlatan—a cheaper material than ours—but that was because they were used only for one performance or, at the most, two. Their feather-weight tu-tu's have four skirts, gathered very full—compared with the fourteen to sixteen skirts I used to wear in the ballet at Covent Garden— and there is an extra frill over the pants. The tu-tu's are made without a whale-bone hoop, so the partner can come in close to the ballerina with ease. The total result is to give the ballerina much greater freedom of movement.

The basques come low over the hips so that the line of the body is never cluttered up. The bodices, cut low at the back, are always well shaped. I noticed that the costumes were invariably made of very beautiful materials with lovely colourings. Typical was the fact that the feathers on the shoulders and head-dresses of the *corps de ballet* of swan-maidens as well as those of Odette, were all real feathers.

I was not so impressed, however, with the men's costumes. The short trunks which they wore over their tights and under their short tunics seemed to be ridiculous because they just added extra lines and looked old-fashioned. I never could find out whether these were worn because of Puritanism or tradition. In any case the rule could sometimes be broken because, to take one example, the Spanish dancers in *Swan Lake* wore only tights and short tunics.

I had a similar feeling about make-up. The women's was wonderful; the men's mediocre. In the West a woman's beauty is sometimes lessened by her make-up on stage, but in Russia I thought it was exactly the reverse. Yet the men seemed excessively and even coarsely made up, and this was particularly true of those with character parts.

I noticed a difference, too, when I studied the cut of the Russian point shoes. The satin was cut down to more of a V-shape on top, accentuating the line of the instep but also, in my opinion, the big toe-joint as well. The soles of the shoes were much stronger than ours, and this, I am sure, helped them in their long, swift *bourrées*

50

across the vast Bolshoi stage. Generally, the flexibility of their shoes gave them every opportunity to display the suppleness and liveliness of their feet. The shoes felt lighter than those generally made in the West.

Another unusual feature was the prompter active in the wings. He read the script and made certain that the dancers were making the proper entrances and exits. Another official—an ex-dancer—was in the wings to act as *regisseur*. Part of his job was to see that ballerinas and soloists were called individually from their dressing-rooms.

But these were all physical differences. A difference which seemed to me on a different plane—almost a spiritual one—was in the orchestra. How I loved dancing with the Bolshoi musicians! They were all first-class players, and it was a fantastic experience to appear with this wonderful orchestra. What interested me particularly was the way in which the conductor brought out all the brass and the wood-winds without fear of overwhelming the strings, giving Tchaikovsky, for instance, added drama.

Rehearsals are always attended by the conductor, and there seem to be far more pianists than at home. New choreography is taught by music; counting is rarely used. Any step I wished to repeat, however short the sequence, was always accompanied by music.

How does one become a Bolshoi dancer? And what lies ahead for him? The process, which in most cases begins at the age of nine or ten, is surely the most elaborate ballet-training system in the world.

The Bolshoi system is helped by two things: first, the unstinted State support to which I have already referred; and, secondly, the fact that the prestige and security attaching to a dancer's life in Russia make it possible to draw recruits from a much wider field than in Britain. It is a brave or confident parent here who would encourage, say, his son to take up dancing as a career. In Russia circumstances are different.

At the Bolshoi School alone there are between 1,000 and 1,500 applicants for places each year. Of these, fewer than sixty are accepted. Trainees are classified in three groups, of which the most important is that in which training starts at about nine years old and lasts until the age of nineteen. This group produces most of the best

51

classical dancers. Then there are children who join between twelve and thirteen. They rarely get Bolshoi employment but provide the dancers in lesser companies. Lastly, there are the thirteen- and fourteen-year-olds who almost invariably train to become character dancers, often joining dance groups and circuses.

Once a child has been accepted the parents are not allowed to interfere in any way with the training. The dangers arising from an over-eager mother's desire to see a fully-fledged ballerina at the end of the first year is thus avoided. Every year each dancer's abilities are re-assessed and many are switched from their original group to the one more suited to their development; while others are dismissed and returned to outside schools to pursue a different career.

I thought it particularly sensible that, though the emphasis at the school is naturally placed on dancing, general education is taken just as seriously. As in the majority of our ballet schools which combine general education and dancing, all pupils take the normal school-leaving certificate around sixteen; and, if it turns out that they are unlikely to have a useful career in ballet, it is easy to switch them into another profession. Besides one and a half hours of classical ballet every day of a six-day week, there are also classes in character dancing, national dancing, traditional mime, historical dancing, *pas-de-deux* training, and make-up.

The student gains stage experience in operas and ballets, such as *The Sleeping Beauty*, where children are needed. Generally he is used in Bolshoi productions from the age of thirteen—and sometimes even earlier. This means he gradually learns the current repertoire of the company.

As the pupil gets older, he takes part in the few public performances given yearly by the school in the smaller Bolshoi Filial Theatre. These are important events in the life of the Moscow ballet fan, for here it is possible to spot a potential star.

After he has taken his school-leaving certificate his last two years at the Bolshoi School include concentrated study of the history of ballet, fine arts, music, and the theatre.

Finally he leaves school able to play at least one instrument well. Yuri, for instance, had specialised in the piano, as we discovered whenever we had a dull moment during our tour and he found himself near one. The piano is also my instrument, but the difference

52

27. The Prince raising the exhausted Odette after her struggle with the Magician. Act IV, *Swan Lake*, at the Bolshoi.

28. With Kondratov and full *corps de ballet* in the climax towards the end of Act IV, *Swan Lake*, at the Bolshoi.

29. Final curtain call on my opening night at the Bolshoi.

30. After my opening night at the Bolshoi. *Left to right:* Golovkina, Plisetskaya, Kondratov, Beryl Grey, Faier, Levashev, Struchkova, and Messerer.

31. Mrs Chulaki and
Sulamith Messerer in
the director's box at the
Bolshoi.

32. Yuri Faier, chief conductor, with Chulaki, director of the Bolshoi, after my first performance.

33. With Chaboukiani after his performance as Othello in Tiflis.

is that I had to learn it privately. This musical insistence at the Bolshoi School is of use in more ways than one. At Kiev, for instance, the conductor of the orchestra is a former dancer, and an ex-ballerina conducts at one of the Leningrad companies.

All the dancers I met seemed to be extremely well-treated. One thing the Bolshoi dancers have which would be highly attractive to most people throughout the British theatre: the certainty of a pension after twenty years. It is not necessary, of course, to retire then. Many dancers continue—like the great Ulanova. Others I met who were on pension and still devoting their enormous talents to the ballet included Semeyonova, Gerdt, Messerer, and Lavrovsky, now choreographers and teachers.

Outside Moscow there is a rest home for all at the Bolshoi to use for week-ends and holidays. It is in beautiful country, where it is possible to swim, sail, and fish. Indoor games are provided also, such as billiards and table tennis. All artists and scientists in general are given preferential treatment regarding holidays. Travel and financial arrangements are taken care of by the government so that the Bolshoi artist has the benefit of these "homes" and watering places, in various parts of the Soviet Union.

While in Moscow I was invited twice into the homes of dancers, but as I fell ill at the time, I could not go, much to my disappointment. However, they were clearly a privileged section of the community. There were many splendid fur coats backstage and—even more significant, in view of the drab displays in the shops—women dancers wore pretty coloured underwear.

If Soviet dancers are well treated by the Bolshoi, so was I. I was not only impressed by the warmth of their welcome but also by their genuine interest in the British ballet. They were anxious to find out as much as they could about how we did things; and there was no slavishness about their tradition. They thought nothing of altering a position or a sequence to suit the style of a dancer if it expressed the ballet correctly. Because the Bolshoi is so confident—and that is quite different from being arrogant—it is all the more prepared to be flexible artistically. That is something I have not always found in Western theatres.

## Chapter VII

## *SOVIET DANCERS AT WORK*

ONE of the outstanding differences between dancers in Russia and dancers in the West is in their carriage. The Russians carry themselves superbly. It is even a thrill to see them standing at the bar in class.

If I had known nothing about their training, it would still have been easy to guess that it had been most careful and thorough, and that they had been given every chance to train slowly.

All the dancers seem to have a mastery over body and temperament. I was told that enormous attention is paid right from the start to the training of body posture; and this, with a complete turn-out, is mastered before too many ballet *enchaînements* are taught.

Thus the repertoire of ballet is built upon a sound foundation, while at the same time self-expression is encouraged. As a result you get a definite style—the arched back and the striking bearing are almost the Russian hall-mark—yet each dancer shows great individuality and feeling.

In company classes all dancers are shown the same *enchaînement*, but the interpretation of the steps is left to the individual. That is what provides a great deal of the colour in Soviet ballet. I got the impression that the dancer's interpretations grew genuinely from within. Certainly they appeared to be deeply felt and carried conviction with all the audiences I watched.

The absorption in their interpretation spills over naturally into their everyday lives. During my short stay I realised how much time and thought was given to the further development of their roles. They would discuss them for hours—not so much from the technical approach as from the interpretative.

54

It seemed that the technical mastery of dancers at the peak was such that they could concentrate more and more on the portrayal of the roles and infuse each movement with greater meaning.

Personally, I applauded this individuality of interpretation, which is not confined to the performer but also extends to the choreographer. It was a pleasure to note the flexibility of thought in producers who would take infinite care to create a step or a movement to suit the characteristic style of the artist. I believe that by such an attitude dancer and ballet both benefit.

In the West you often find two extremes—either a rigidity of mind and unwillingness to admit any change in choreography; or, alternatively, a complete disregard for the original conception, which sometimes results in the mutilation of an entire classic. Both these attitudes are dangerous. To be bound slavishly by tradition is often to stagnate. But by building on a tradition one has the opportunity of drawing from a masterpiece while recognising that such features as the artist, size of stage, company resources, and so on, must often differ with each production.

The arched back of the Russian dancer produces a beautifully lifted chest. It also seems to make the arms more rounded and expressive and gives them a lift from underneath. All this, in my opinion, comes directly from the control of the spine.

Russian backs are very supple. They remind me of some swords —strong, straight, and flexible. The vital thing, I consider, is their achievement of a very great mobility of the lower back. This enables them to bend forwards, backwards, and sideways in an astonishing manner while still preserving their classical style.

Suppleness would of course be nothing without strong back and stomach muscles, developed from the very beginning of their training. This results in such strength and control over these muscles that no woman ever wears an elastic abdominal belt.

I was impressed too by their control of the upper back. I do not think this comes entirely from the so-called "pulling together of the shoulder-blades", which is often taught over here and which can so easily result in thrust-out ribs. The Russians concentrate more on the muscles farther down the back, and from here they draw a great deal of their strength. (I understand this area is also given great attention in the training of Russian pianists.) In a dancer this control helps to make breathing easier and leads, indeed,

55

to a feeling of more confidence, more command, and more authority.

Control of the back makes for freer movement of the arms, and allows feeling to flow directly from the body to the tips of the fingers. Russian dancers are often accused of flamboyant hands and "broken" wrists. This is true of some, but it seems to me to be preferable to the stiff arm, or the taut hand pointing away at some odd angle, with which the Russians can counter-accuse us.

In fact the Russian use of arms and hands thrilled me time and again throughout my visit. They used them to finish a movement or accentuate a dramatic point with the maximum amount of feeling, and musicality.

No step in class, however simple, is given without an accompanying head and body movement. This, I thought, gave added point and style to their work. At the same time it prevented the stiff neck and body which one sees so often in ballet dancers in the West. The Russians appear to have a natural flow of movement through the entire body.

Their turn-out was always fine and strong. The legs were well pulled up and straight, and the body appeared to be well up on the hips. Their extensions were generally high.

In class I was surprised to find that it was chiefly the straight-leg *arabesques* which were given. There were comparatively few of the bent-knee *arabesques* which most of us in the West consider to be particularly theirs. Incidentally, it is often thought that the bent type is an easier and more relaxed way of doing an *arabesque*. Personally, I found it harder, as it should be done with a very high leg extension and good turn-out.

In both a "bent" and a "straight" *arabesque* great attention is paid at the Bolshoi to the turn-out. The hip of the lifted leg is often raised to allow the leg to be better turned, thus avoiding the knee falling below the line of the leg, which is not so attractive.

Their "straight" *arabesques* are actually drawn more in the shape of a bow than in the rigid straight line generally seen in the West. This, I think, is explained by the Russian ability to bend backwards in the lower spine. At the same time their knees are usually quite flattened, and the line is enhanced by the complete turn-out of the stretched foot.

Many times, I remember, Semeyonova would check that my

56

knee was completely tight and take my foot and mould it round into this position. The arch of the *arabesque* was thus intensified, and I found here how important it was to have those strong back muscles for a position such as this. For a particularly dramatic line, however, a slight bending of the knee is occasionally allowed.

The feet of Russian dancers are particularly alive. Never did I see a Russian sickle a foot. They use their feet expressively; but, as in the West, one sometimes sees dancers who are not completely "up" on their full *pointes*.

Nobody who saw the Russians in London during the Bolshoi visit could forget their amazing *bourrées*. They covered the stage on full point with a speed which I had never seen equalled before. Their *bourrées* were even more impressive in Moscow when they were performed over a much larger area.

It was the same with their "runs". In London, people speak to this day of the way Ulanova ran in *Romeo and Juliet*. Indeed, she and many of her fellow-dancers hardly appeared to touch the ground, conveying a superb excitement and urgency. In *Swan Lake*, for instance, I found the whole *corps de ballet* possessed this same characteristic. I attributed this in part to their ability to lean well forward from the hips as they run, thereby facilitating rapid leg movements.

I was not so happy about the Russian walk. In the middle of a beautiful performance many of the classical dancers—even the ballerinas—would suddenly adopt an unattractive, slightly square walk.

Their elevation is exciting. The strength of their legs and feet no doubt has a lot to do with this. When they jump they appear to leave the ground more quickly and more strongly than many Western dancers. When they land they are helped also by the strength of their body muscles, which enables them to hold a position firmly and without wobbling. This is true of both men and women.

I noticed that in the men's jumps and *pirouettes* a very high percentage turned to the left. In Act I of the *Sleeping Beauty*, for instance, three of the four cavaliers turned to the left and only one to the right, which was slightly disturbing from in front! I believe that Messerer used to perform turns equally well to the left and to the right.

57

The women are also capable of spectacular jumps and turns. These were so popular—the Russian public, like audiences the world over, revels in them—that I was surprised to see the famous thirty-two *fouettés* omitted from Act III of *Swan Lake*. In the performance I saw Plisetskaya substituted two *piqué* turns and four *chaînés*. These, incidentally, proved to me that the Russians do give *chaînés* on full point on stage as well as in class.

However, in the last Act of *The Sleeping Beauty*, *fouettés* were performed by the ballerina—for me an interesting innovation.

The common belief in England is that the Russians work far harder than we do and that their training is much tougher. This did not appear to me to be the case. Their company classes, for instance, are only one hour, like ours. (Many classes in London and Paris studios are one and a half and two hours.) It is true that they have some athletic types, but so does every company; most of the women, on stage, were elegant and feminine.

One of my strongest impressions was of the polish and finish among even the youngest dancers. There were surprisingly few corrections necessary in class. Instead, there was an atmosphere of deeply professional concentration, with everybody knowing quite clearly what result was wanted. There was complete calmness and no unnecessary noise.

I did not observe any compulsion about doing every exercise, and a dancer who wished to leave class early did so. Discipline seemed to be left very much to the dancer's own discretion and sense. On the other hand, one must remember that any dancer who has got that far must be by that time a dedicated person.

I liked the women's practice clothes. They have long tunics, usually transparent, of soft flowing material. These are knee-length and the dancers tuck them up above their legs when necessary. I also liked their bodices, which were cut low at the back, with narrow shoulder-straps. I had one of these tunics made for me before I left for Russia, and I must say it gave me a wonderful freedom of movement. Brown woollen leggings were often worn over their pink tights for added warmth to the legs. Many of the men, on the other hand, often worked in class in trousers fitted at the ankles, though some wore tights. Messerer always led his class in trousers, and Yuri almost always rehearsed in them.

Men and women often work in the same class. Character dancers also attend ballet classes appropriate to their position in the company, and not according to their classical dancing abilities. So it is not unusual to see character dancers working side by side with leading ballerinas.

I was surprised to see many of the older artists were still taking part in daily classes. This says much for the soundness of their basic training. I think another probable reason is that the average Russian dancer takes part in far fewer performances a year than his counterpart in the West. There is always a place in the Soviet ballet for the older dancers. There are numerous acting roles to which their maturity and long experience add authenticity.

Russian male dancers are justly famous for their virility. They bring to every performance an uncompromising masculine quality often lacking in ballet in the West. The result of this attitude is to complement and emphasise the femininity of the ballerina. There is thus a realism about Russian productions which reveals how meretricious are the so-called "sex ballets" which are occasionally staged with such publicity outside the Soviet Union.

Virility is one reason why Russian men, in my experience, make the best partners. Their work is characterised at all times by great assurance and ease in handling their ballerinas.

Allied to their strength is a sensitivity in the guiding and control of the ballerina. This comes from an innate understanding of her placing and timing.

First with Chaboukiani in practice, and then with Kondratov for a whole month, I always felt that my partner was the master—and with mastery over himself as well as the ballerina. I had absolute confidence in whatever choreography was demanded.

A Russian partner generally stands a long way from his ballerina. This allows her exceptional freedom of movement. He also has strong balance, and there is never any sensation of unsteadiness.

Yuri, too, always seemed to sense ahead what I was going to do —and if it was wrong in those anxious early days, he was able to correct me. He not only provided support but directed as well.

What was interesting was the way a partner would guide a ballerina's body in any direction by the placing of one hand and even by the mere pressure of his thumb. Through this control he could dictate, for instance, the height of the ballerina's leg. This

59

was of enormous help, as I found my leg springing a few inches higher and, what is more, staying there.

. Yuri also would alter the position of the hip of the ballerina's raised leg when necessary to enhance the beauty of a line or to facilitate a smoother choreographic arrangement. It was exciting the way he would project me into an off-balance position to give a particular line or feeling to a part.

In Russia I found that the ballerina is of first importance to the cavalier, her presentation in the best possible way being his major consideration. I noticed in my partner complete absence of rush and anxiety. Yet always he seemed to be in the right position without hurry, and I sensed in him a feeling of quiet confidence at all times. He possessed and passed on to me that sense of disciplined timelessness which pervaded the whole Russian ballet.

During my work on *Swan Lake* and *Giselle* I learned many Russian lifts which were quite new to me. From these their tremendous strength and mastery of the technique of partnership was apparent. Here again I realised why they place such importance on those back and stomach muscles.

Yuri, in fact, symbolised in many ways the whole of the Russian ballet. Before an entrance he would never talk. Instead, he would walk up and down in the wings, never catching anybody's eye, always apparently deep in thought. Obviously he was listening to the music and steeping himself in his role. Like most of the others, he would not practise before going on. There was never much talking in the wings by anybody in the company. Instead, all would be completely dedicated to the perfection of the performance.

This was the atmosphere I had hoped to find when I came to dance in Russia. So often in life one is disappointed. But in this instance I found that, if anything, I had under-estimated the drive towards perfection.

I have deliberately written at some length on technical things. But I cannot emphasise enough that in the final product on stage one is conscious first and foremost of dancing; and that technique, having been mastered, is subservient to the portrayal of the role.

34. With Kondratov in *Giselle* at Tiflis. The first meeting with Albrecht in Act I.

35. *Giselle* at Tiflis. With Kondratov at the end of the first big dance with the village girls in Ac[

36. As Giselle in Act I at the Maryinsky Theatre, Leningrad.

37. *Giselle*, Act I, at Leningrad. The moment of doubt.

38. *Giselle*, Act I, at Leningrad. The moment of betrayal.

Chapter VIII

## *FIFTEEN RED STARS*

HIGH among the special characteristics of Russian dancers is their obvious lack of self-consciousness both on and off the stage. That was one of the reasons why it was such a pleasure to work with them. This lack of self-consciousness leads to a complete absence of affectation in their private lives as well as in their work. I think this is largely because dancing is such an integral part of Russian lives. In Britain a dancer is usually regarded as a person apart, but in the Soviet Union an artist is as much a part of the national life as any footballer or cricketer in this country.

That is not to say that somebody like Ulanova lives a Denis Compton-like existence. Indeed by Western standards the leading dancers in Russia get surprisingly little publicity. They are certainly able to lead almost cloistered private lives. It appears they are photographed quite rarely. I found it difficult to obtain even one photograph of Yuri Kondratov though Sven and I asked for pictures of him frequently. Eventually we were given six photographs of him in *Giselle*—all in the same position!

Although the star system exists in Russia, it operates on a very different scale from our own. I saw no names of dancers on posters. The fans always seem to know when a great dancer such as Ulanova or Plisetskaya is dancing, but they have a grape-vine of their own. For the outsider it was most difficult to find who was dancing the leading roles at any performance, and this was one of the complaints I heard frequently from fellow-countrymen, staying at the various Moscow hotels, who got their tickets through Intourist. The rank of the artists can be judged by the title which follows an important name in the Soviet Union. The highest of the three which can be given is "People's Artist of the U.S.S.R."

This is held by Ulanova, Lepeshinskaya, and Chaboukiani, for example. Below this is "People's Artist of the R.S.F.S.R." (or whichever republic is appropriate), held by Plisetskaya, Struchkova, and Messerer. The lowest award is "Honoured Artist of the R.S.F.S.R." (or other republics), held by Kondratov, Lapauri, and Bovt. As would be expected in a company the size of the Bolshoi, major roles have several exponents. The interpreters range from the youngest dancers of promise to those of an established position.

If I had to sum up in one paragraph what I found in the Soviet ballet, I would say that their dancers possess an amazing technique and fluidity, with a natural feeling for dance, music, and drama. They have an outstanding ability to live their roles. After perfecting their technique they concentrate on introducing touches of light and shade which, coupled with their dynamic strength and breath-taking positions, put them in a position apart from the rest of the ballet world.

I met almost all the leading ballet figures in the Soviet Union, and it is a temptation to write fully about them all, even those of whom I saw little. However, I shall restrict my observations to the personalities with whom I had most to do.

## VACHTANG CHABOUKIANI

One of the greatest male dancers in the world, Chaboukiani in private life is a man of dignity, whose quiet manner conceals his enormous knowledge of his art. He is the only dancer I remember meeting who has a moustache, but in him this seems perfectly in place. A Georgian with all the temperament on stage that one would expect of this wonderful, virile race, he now directs and leads the company at Tiflis of which his dancing is its finest adornment. In his own town he is worshipped in a way in which I think it would be impossible for a dancer in Moscow to be worshipped. I was very happy that he was to be my partner, and was correspondingly disappointed when he had to leave the Bolshoi rehearsals because of a recurrence of the knee trouble which so far has been the only snag in a glittering career which brought him two Stalin prizes and the Lenin Award.

I saw him dance in the second performance of his own ballet,

*Othello,* when he showed himself a great actor. Particularly impressive was his ability to perform a fantastic number of *pirouettes.* He has a fine athletic figure which the audience saw to the best possible advantage in the later scenes when he wore only a small loin-cloth. Now forty-six, his first major choreographic success was in *Heart of the Hills.* Chaboukiani left the Bolshoi six years ago, but he returns there from time to time for special performances.

### NIKOLAI FADEYECHEV

Here is a dancer, in his middle twenties, taller than most, who is of the very highest promise. Still developing, he should stamp his name on the history of ballet in our time. Like so many of the younger dancers at the Bolshoi, he is Moscow-trained, and has already danced the lead in *Swan Lake* and partnered Ulanova in *Giselle.*

He had a considerable success in both these ballets during the Bolshoi visit to London, and I heard when I arrived in Moscow that it had been planned for him to partner me. I should have been most pleased at this, but he had just strained the tendon of a calf-muscle, so it was impossible for him to appear.

Fadeyechev possess a wealth of talent and humility—a combination I noticed time and again in leading Soviet dancers. He has a splendid *balon,* a strong clean technique, and a long, pleasing line.

### YURI FAIER

This gifted conductor of the Bolshoi Ballet Company is now getting on in years, but nothing I could write about his work would be adequate. As a dancer I had never before met a conductor who possessed such a quality for inspiring me or had such an understanding of ballet technique, the ballerina's individual style and tempi, and everything, in fact, that a first-class performance demands. He was at all my rehearsals and his absorption in ballet is such that he frequently watches class as well. I should like very much to work with such a man over a long period.

His private manner is as attractive as his professional one. He is a chubby, short man, with a great geniality of approach and a good nature that nothing seems to alter. Short-sighted now, he sees best at long range. He always greeted me with an all-enveloping embrace and a kiss, and was one of the first people who convinced me that I was welcome and would be helped as much as possible at the Bolshoi. I remember him also for his fur hat—an enormous brown affair, with a very high crown, which was the most magnificent I have ever seen. But almost everything about him is magnificent.

## YURI KONDRATOV

Much as I have already written about him, there is still much to be said before I can express the admiration I feel for this wonderful Russian, who is the best partner I have ever had. He is thirty-six years old, well-built and, though Moscow-born, has a surprisingly dark skin. He has finely shaped legs and excellent feet. Married to an attractive woman who is a TV announcer, he has a daughter aged six. During his first formative years on stage he danced with Semeyonova, and it was with her that he obtained his technique of partnering. Then he danced with Ulanova and accompanied her on her tours in Italy and the Far East. Now he frequently partners Lepeshinskaya, Plisetskaya, and Struchkova.

As a solo dancer one of his outstanding achievements is a double *tour en l'air*, landing on one leg with the other extended behind in *arabesque*. I noticed that he turned most of his *pirouettes*—which usually numbered six—to the left. His generous personality comes over the footlights very well, as I felt on my third night in Moscow when I saw him dance in *Swan Lake* with Plisetskaya. With the ballerina he is quite unassuming and always the perfect cavalier. He performs the most arduous lifts and supports without ever seeming apprehensive or suggesting any difficulty. At rehearsals he is quiet and serious, yet, as in private life, always assured and good-natured.

Kondratov has an attractive wit, and to him I owe a lot of the smoothness with which my rehearsals in the Russian theatres were accomplished. Indeed, throughout our tour, he was always ready to try to avert difficulties, and he was invariably the one responsible for breaking the tension on arrival at a new theatre. Sven and I found him the most charming of travelling companions. I hope to dance with him again, not only because of his superb gifts as a partner but also because I feel that in him we made a personal friend for life.

## ALEXANDER LAPAURI

An outstanding partner, whose powerful physique is well suited to *pas-de-deux* work, Lapauri is a fine artist in his own right. He often appears with his wife, Raisa Struchkova, and is a first-class actor. One of his memorable roles was as the Khan Girei in *The Fountain of Bakhchiserai*. He has recently turned his talents to choreography as well, and is now at work on a short ballet (to Medtner's music) based on Maxim Gorki's story *Danko*. An open-hearted person, his character comes through clearly in performances. Like so many of the Soviet male dancers he is remarkable for the unselfish and effective way in which he presents his ballerina.

## LEONID LAVROVSKY

I first met him when the Bolshoi Company was in London and he visited us in our flat. It was delightful to meet him again in Moscow, for I had always admired his choreography. I was pleased when I found he had come to my first performance at the Bolshoi, and told me he had enjoyed my dancing. Lavrovsky will of course always be remembered for his choreography of *Romeo and Juliet* and *The Red Poppy*. (Incidentally, it is interesting to note that this is now performed in Moscow under the title of *The Red Flower*. I was told this was because the Chinese objected to the poppy's association with opium.) Lavrovsky, in his early fifties, is now teaching at the Moscow Institute of Choreography, and obviously has great influence among the young dancers just beginning to develop their work.

## VLADIMIR A. LEVASHEV

He is typical of the Soviet dancers with whom I worked and whom I grew to like so much. As Von Rothbart the magician in *Swan Lake*, he took enormous pains to have all our double work clearly understood and perfectly executed. About the same age as Yuri, he is one of his friends, and is also married with one small child.

65

I was particularly impressed by his artistry. It seemed impossible for him to make a wrong move, and he always lived his roles, even at rehearsals. Tall, slender, and strong, he lifts extremely well. He has fair hair and is yet another of those Russians whose reticence conceals a most friendly disposition.

## OLGA LEPESHINSKAYA

Born just before the 1917 revolution, she is probably the most politically conscious of the Soviet ballerinas and is, in fact, a member of the Supreme Soviet. She is a few years younger than Ulanova and, like her, is a People's Artist of the Soviet Union. She was away from Moscow recuperating from an illness when I arrived and so I did not meet her until my return. Then I did not recognise her when she followed me to my dressing-room and asked if I would give an interview for a Russian paper for which she wrote. It was not until half-way through our talk that it came out that she was the famous Lepeshinskaya. She asked for two pictures of myself—one for her paper and one for her to keep. She was anxious for me to see her dance in *Laurencia* on January 10th, and it was a big disappointment that I had to leave for home before then. Short and strongly built, Lepeshinskaya is famed for her dazzling technique and vivacious personality.

## ASAF MESSERER

Now ballet-master and choreographer at the Bolshoi, he was one of Russia's most brilliant male dancers. Messerer is about forty-six, possesses tremendous vitality, and has a deep love for the dance, taking delight in demonstrating his own choreography. Short in height, with expressive arms, he had at his peak a fantastic elevation. During all my days in the theatre he was an enormous help to me.

Messerer gives one of the top classes and has among his pupils Ulanova, Struchkova, Zdhanov, Koren, and Lapauri. He leads the principals in his own class, dancing all the steps himself and giving corrections when necessary.

Married to the ballerina Irina Tikhomirnova, he is one of the

66

few at the Bolshoi who speaks a little English. I adored working with him, as he is a stimulating personality and a very clear teacher, with whom I felt *en rapport* at once. He is a kind and warm-hearted man, and I sensed during my stay that all the dancers loved him.

### SULAMITH MESSERER

Asaf Messerer's sister Sulamith is a graduate of the Moscow school, unlike most of the Bolshoi teachers of her generation. She, too, was an outstanding dancer and is rather short, with black hair and dark eyes, and resembles her brother in friendliness of manner. I watched her taking a class with soloists when her method might have been a model for teachers anywhere. She took such trouble with each one that every dancer must have felt that his or her work· was Sulamith's only concern in life.

### MAYA PLISETSKAYA

She is a niece of the Messerers—really, it seems impossible to keep away from this gifted family! I was particularly interested in her, for she is about my own age, of comparable physique, and people had been kind enough to say that we had much in common. She is certainly one of the tallest of Soviet ballerinas. Her face is full of character. Obviously born to be a ballerina, on stage she has the most compelling personality.

I shall never forget her performance in *Swan Lake*. There was a superb vivacity and attack in Act III, while in Acts II and IV she had all the remoteness and poetic quality one could desire. Above all, I shall remember her expressive arms and the way they undulated on her exit at the end of Act II. One could see the metamorphosis from woman to swan actually happening on stage in front of one's eyes. She has a very high extension, with a breath-taking jump, and is famous for her *jetés* when she leaps high into the air with her legs stretched into one long curved line, her body leaning backwards over the back leg.

Personally we were in sympathy from our first meeting and in every way she tried to give me the benefit of her professional experience. She even used her own instrument—which in fact was a fish-scaler freely adapted to the ballerina's requirement—to

67

scrape my ballet shoes to prevent them from slipping; and she lent me her own special hammer for breaking down the blocks of the point shoes. One of the most striking artists I have seen, she is a good actress as well as dancer, and altogether an enchanting personality.

## VADIM RINDIN

The chief designer at the Bolshoi, Vadim Rindin, who in private life is the husband of Ulanova, is known for his *décor* for *Romeo and Juliet* and other famous Bolshoi works. I sat next to him at the British Embassy party after my first Moscow performance and found him, like many other Russians, shy but charming. He touched me by his efforts to speak English and make me feel at home. It was most interesting to hear his account of his wife's recent entry into choreography with the new ballet *Joan of Arc* at the Stanislavsky Theatre. They live in a skyscraper block of apartments on the banks of the River Moscow—a most imposing building, which dominates that part of the city.

## MARINA SEMEYONOVA

I cannot write enough of this famous dancer, wonderful teacher, and generous friend. She has lovely dark eyes in a round Slav face, and these really did light up when she smiled—which was often. She has the tiniest feet and the most expressive arms I have ever seen.

Semeyonova is a very careful and kind producer, but also very critical. She sets an extremely high standard and no detail escapes her either at rehearsal or performance. I liked to watch her demonstrating the various swan movements when her arms seemed almost to dissolve. It has been said that the Russians do not pay enough attention to the hands, but she spotted at once when my hands were strained or my wrists bent. I liked her ways of working: corrections were given quietly but always with understanding, naturalness, and warmth. Never rehearsing me unduly and always watching for any tell-tale sign of tiredness or strain, she seemed to understand the mental anxiety inseparable from a first performance in a foreign country. At the Bolshoi, she was adored

68

39. Chaboukiani as the Moor and Kikaleishvili as Iago in *Othello* at Tiflis.

Violetta Bovt in the
role of the ballet
*nne d'Arc*.

41. The third form of the Bolshoi Theatre's Ballet School at work under Lidia Rafaikova.

42. Three ballerinas practising at the Bolshoi. *Left to right:* E. Farmanyants, G. Ulanova, I. Tikhomirnova.

43. As Odette, with Kondratov as the Prince, Act IV, *Swan Lake*, at Kiev, showing the happy ending and the head-dresses lying on the stage.

44. With Lepeshinskaya and Kondratov after my final performance at the Bolshoi. In the background are Semeyonova, Tomski, and Chulaki.

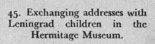

45. Exchanging addresses with Leningrad children in the Hermitage Museum.

by everybody, and they all seemed sad that she no longer danced herself. She was one of their greatest ballerinas. I should have known that at once even if I had never heard of her before.

### RAISA STRUCHKOVA

She is married to Lapauri who often partners her. I had met this talented couple when they were in London, so it was like meeting old friends to find them again in Moscow. She is very fond of children but has none of her own. Her dressing-table is covered with photographs of children—including one, I was happy to see, of my own son.

Struchkova was a star from her graduation and on stage almost bubbles over with the joy of dancing. She has beautifully arched feet and strong shapely legs. There is charm and nobility in her bearing and there seems no end to her technical accomplishments, including the very difficult Russian arrangement of the *Rose Adage* in *The Sleeping Beauty*. Already beloved by English audiences, she dances most of Ulanova's roles, having recently added *Giselle* to her repertoire with great success.

### GALINA ULANOVA

Last in this alphabetical list of those dancers I had the good fortune to know in Russia, Ulanova is first in the estimation of ballet-lovers all over the world. What can I say about this legendary figure that has not already been written? How can I describe the impression she has made on all who have seen her dance? I was not fortunate enough to see one of her performances in Moscow, though I met her frequently. But I shall always remember the lyric quality of her dancing in London. And always, too, I shall be amazed at the change from her off-stage personality—quiet, dignified, yet perhaps not one's idea of a dancer—into her dancing personality. In private life it is the eyes, perhaps, which give the clue. They have a piercing blueness which do not seem altogether of this world—like her dancing. It is the same in class as on the stage. Whenever she dances she becomes light, supple, young—a girl in her 'teens again. There is the most perfect fluidity in which dance, poetry, drama, and music are all blended. Indeed, she does seem to make music visible. There is no more one can say.

69

Chapter IX

# IT WAS ALL SO DIFFERENT

I HAD expected to find differences between the Russian and British versions of the two ballets I was to dance, but I had not realised that there would be so many.

It was only on that first Sunday evening, when I watched *Swan Lake* at the Bolshoi, that I appreciated fully the difficulties which lay ahead. That feeling was submerged almost at once by an ever more compelling impression—a feeling of the greatness of *Swan Lake* as given by the Bolshoi Company in their own theatre.

How much better it was in Moscow than when I saw the smaller Russian company dance it in London! At the Bolshoi the vast sets and the wonderful stage effects intensified and added to the dramatic moments. The lighting was also better than in London, particularly in Act III. It was interesting that when I danced these lights, though very bright, did not blind me or upset my balance, as has happened in Western theatres.

I was fortunate, of course, to see Plisetskaya, one of the outstanding contemporary dancers, appear that night as Odette-Odile. What a joy it was to see her, what a joy to watch a company travelling across the stage with such controlled abandon, and what a joy to realise that I, too, was soon to become a member of that enchanted group.

I was pleased for personal reasons to be dancing first in *Swan Lake*, as it is a ballet which has been associated with some of the most memorable moments of my career. It is difficult to realise, thinking of it today, that when it was first performed in 1877 it was a failure. The story of *Swan Lake* has in fact already provided a whole book by Cyril Beaumont. The present choreography is by A. A. Gorski and Asaf Messerer, based on that by Petipa-Ivanov.

70

For me the main differences between the Bolshoi and Covent Garden versions lay in the mime scenes. These were almost entirely eliminated in Moscow and dancing substituted, which often contained elegant *arabesques* and simple poetic arrangements, all expressing the music and helping the story.

Act II having been re-staged, all the groupings and patterns of the swans were different, even including their first entrance, which in this version came before the Swan Queen's. Even the *pas de deux* in Act II between Odette and Siegfried had in some parts a different pattern and direction.

In Moscow, Von Rothbart played a more significant part, and the audience was made fully aware of his power over Odette and Odile. There were no huntsmen accompanying the prince, so the moment when the swans assemble in fear of being shot did not come. They were in a different place on the stage, and the Swan Queen did not appear for their protection, but to look for the prince.

I thought the absence of Benno, the prince's friend, was a great improvement. In the West he plays an important part in the famous *pas de deux*, but I have always thought this somewhat distracting, for it is surely more convincing as an expression of love when danced by only two people. I was told that Benno's part was only put in because the original Siegfried was a man of fifty who needed some relief from the strain imposed by the long, exacting *pas de deux*! In Act I instead of Benno the Bolshoi version had a court jester who also appears in Act III. Particularly impressive was the long, slow lift of the ballerina by the prince in Act II, shortly before she is drawn away by Von Rothbart.

In Act III the dramatic impact of Odile was intensified by the way in which the *divertissements* are arranged to lead up to her first appearance. After that first entrance she has only to wait for one more *divertissement*—the Spanish Dance, which is the most brilliant and exciting of all the numbers. This makes a perfect lead into the famous Black Swan *pas de deux*, which is always eagerly anticipated by the public.

The Russian arrangement of this *pas de deux* is almost entirely different from ours. Though I learned it fully later, Semeyonova was insistent that for our performances Yuri and I should follow as nearly as possible my Western version. She suggested several

71

alterations to the Act II *pas de deux*, however, adding little touches which she thought would enhance my interpretation, and which I could absorb thoroughly in the short time available before the opening. My solos, of course, were not altered in any way, apart from some help given in their execution.

Act IV I had to re-learn entirely. It had completely different choreography, including a spectacular *pas de deux* for Odette with the magician, and some beautiful supported work with the prince, The groupings of the *corps de ballet* and their numerous exits and entrances towards the latter part of this act heightened the drama effectively. Much use was made of the swan-like movements here. The choreography had been done skilfully by Messerer, so that it did not seem out of harmony in any way with the choreography of Gorski but rather appeared a natural extension of his work in Act II. The ending of the last act was quite different from any I had seen. The prince fought the magician and broke off one of his wings. With his power lost, the magician died and the spell was broken. The swan-maidens were released and regained their human forms. Odette and the prince were united.

I found almost all the mime had been eliminated in this act. So, with the added music and dancing, the Moscow version of *Swan Lake* became an even greater feat of endurance than that familiar to ballerinas in the West.

All this extra work had to be done on the stage where size also took extra physical toll, as well as the fact that one was expected to cover it at a much greater speed than is customary on Western stages. So I must admit that I was a little relieved, on arriving at Kiev, to find that the last act there was shorter, and had music nearer the version we dance in London. With the prospect of dancing three *Swan Lakes* in five days, there was relief to find that the stage was also smaller than at the Bolshoi.

One of the many changes I noticed in the Kiev ballet was the *pas de trois* in Act I, here danced by two women and two men, thus making it a *pas de quatre*. The opening of Act II was different too, and the harp cadenza leading into my *pas de deux* was the longest and the strangest I have ever heard in my life. It just did not fit the usual choreography.

In Act III the order of *divertissements* differed and included a dance I had never seen. Immediately before the Black Swan *pas*

72

*de deux*, there was an extra number by the magician with a small group of dancers. In my opinion this was far too long and dull, musically and choreographically, and detracted considerably from the dramatic expectancy.

For the happy ending of the last act both companies used the same music, but at Kiev the swan-maidens took off their feathered head-dresses as a symbol of their release from enchantment. Again I preferred the Moscow version, for the sight of all those head-dresses littering the floor symbolised to me untidiness rather than release!

*Giselle*, the other ballet I danced in the Soviet Union, had fewer big changes. It followed the general framework I knew, with some extra music, part of which is used also at the Paris Opera House. So there was only a little additional dancing to learn.

The production ran longer than in the West, and at the Bolshoi and in Tiflis it made a whole evening's entertainment. The interval was long, and the actual ballet ran for an extra twenty minutes. At Leningrad, however, *Giselle* was usually preceded by a shorter work, such as *Chopiniana*.

The great acting ability of the Russian dancers brings out effectively the drama and pathos of the story of *Giselle*. Although the dancing was much the same everywhere, there were many little differences all the way through—steps done the other way round, for instance, or in another direction. In many ways a series of minor alterations is even trickier than major changes.

What was very different from London was the opening mime scene with Albrecht. The whole action was more realistic. I liked also the increased speed of the *ballotés* in Act I. All the jumps done with the partner were taken more quickly and, because they were not so heavy, seemed more in character.

When the music is played too slowly, in my opinion it destroys the lightness and gaiety which *Giselle* should convey, and also shows up the weakness of the score. The music is wonderful to dance to but is not recognised as one of the world's masterpieces, when considered purely as music.

In Act I, I liked particularly the moment of brief hesitation when Giselle stood between Mother and Albrecht, uncertain whom to follow. Then, still a little frightened, in awe of being in love, she went to her mother.

I also liked the way in which the mother tried to protect Giselle from the gamekeeper Hilarion's disclosure that her lover was of royal birth: and the way, too, in which Hilarion himself is shown not as a villain but as a young man ardently in love with Giselle.

The biggest changes in choreography came in Act II, where there were some very expressive lifts with the partner holding the ballerina overhead on his fully stretched arms. There was also a delicate and difficult passage, of little lifts on to full point into *arabesque*, across stage, from small *demi-plies* in fifth position.

In Tiflis and Leningrad they used the older ending with extra music, which was quite unknown to me. A bed of roses came up slowly from the stage and the ballerina was carried to it by Albrecht and laid there gently. In Leningrad the bed sank gradually down. But in Tiflis there was even more music, when, in three conventional mime gestures, she gave her blessing to his marriage with the princess. After this she slowly disappeared from view, down into the underworld of trap-doors, stage supports, and cheering stage-hands!

Personally I much preferred Moscow's less old-fashioned version where Giselle simply *bourrée-d* backwards from Albrecht into the wings, reappearing for a brief moment to throw him a flower.

The stage effects of Act II as they affected Giselle herself are worth mentioning. In Russia these were obviously a much-loved part of the ballet and always produced much appreciation in the audience.

Giselle's first appearance in this act, as one would have expected, was by trap-door. She stood on this in the classical position on one foot with the other resting behind on point. But in Leningrad particularly there was what seemed an excessive use of paraphernalia.

There was a lot of peering through imitation bushes and running up artificial hills and even being pulled across the back of the stage at breakneck speed on a small trolley. This had a leg-holder, which provided the support for the ballerina to lean against so she would be seen eventually poised in a high, tilted, and utterly dangerous *arabesque*! I always foresaw disaster here and also in a later ordeal, when I had to dash up twelve steps and thrust myself

74

breathlessly on to a tree-branch, also complete with hidden metal foot-holder and hip-rester, which was immediately tipped to what I thought was a perilous angle! Standing on one leg in *arabesque*, I then dropped flowers to Albrecht waiting hopefully beneath. After all this I was manœuvred back to the starting-point for the process to be repeated. Then I had to dash down the stairs on to the stage and run up the three steps in front of the grave, only to be lowered swiftly underground again on the trap-door. I felt the patrons were getting their roubles-worth that night!

In Leningrad the company was almost as large as the Bolshoi, but the stage was considerably smaller. The surface of this was not in good condition. Backstage, too, there was none of the spaciousness of the Bolshoi. There was a maze of dark and rather small dressing-rooms, and I was told that lack of space was one of the big handicaps for the theatre as a whole. Company classes, in fact, had to be held in the school building some distance away. But in front the theatre was quite breath-takingly beautiful, both the proportions and the blue, white, and gold colour scheme. The audience, too, seemed better dressed than in Moscow.

The Leningrad ballet-mistress, Zlatkovskaya, was a wonderful help to me, and so also was Elena Liukom, by whom I had the privilege of being produced. She was a contemporary of Tamara Karsavina and danced *Giselle* at the Maryinsky at the same time that Karsavina was dancing there. She inquired tenderly after Karsavina and seemed thrilled when I told her she was still a leading and much-loved figure in the British ballet world.

I, too, was thrilled at my meeting with Liukom. She seemed to be a piece of the history of her own Maryinsky Theatre, suddenly come to life. Today she is a little woman, frail-looking, with completely white hair. But then, suddenly, to demonstrate a point, she will leap across the stage with enormous *jetés*, and one realises what a great dancer she must have been. And one gets again that sense of continuity which the Russian ballet is constantly providing.

75

Chapter X

## WHAT I FOUND IN RUSSIA

THIRTY-TWO days of life in hotels, theatres, aeroplanes, and trains are an interesting introduction to a country, but they certainly do not qualify one to become an expert. Hence I can only give my opinion on the ballet. My other comments on things Russian must necessarily be considered as products of the camera's-eye technique.

Aeroplanes played a big part in my tour. I am not an enthusiastic air traveller at the best of times. My ears in particular are consistently anti-aeroplane. So the most trying aspect of the visit was the travelling.

There is a completely different attitude to air travel in Russia. In a Western plane you are constantly having meals and drinks and magazines pressed on you by pretty hostesses. I think the idea is to keep you occupied and persuaded that you are not really in an aeroplane at all. But there is nothing of this in the Soviet Union. To the Russians a plane is a plane.

We flew on the internal routes in Ilyushin 14's. These are sturdy planes, and certainly they seemed to fulfil the essential function of staying up and getting you from place to place.

The air hostesses were also sturdy. They did not have special uniforms and their function was difficult to determine, as no meals or drinks were served. Smoking was allowed even during take-off and landing. There were safety belts usually but nobody used them.

The hotels we liked. They were always clean. If one ran one's fingers over the tops of doors, one never found dirt. Sheets and towels were changed every day. The *décor* was old-fashioned by our standards, but against that we always had masses of space.

Food was also plentiful, but I did not care for it as a whole, as it was generally more greasy than in the West and there were only a few kinds of fruits and vegetables at that time of year. But we were judging it by our standards and our stomachs. The Russians seemed to like it very well—and, after all, it is their country and climate, and presumably the food suits them.

Of course, we were favoured visitors, living in hotels run largely for foreigners. What about the ordinary people?

I can only report that there seemed plenty of food-shops, and those we visited were well stocked. There were hams, cheeses and fats, and stacks of breads, tinned goods, sausages, and wines. These food-shops were always crowded by people who appeared to have the money to buy fairly freely.

Curious was the amount of ice-cream eaten in the streets even during the sub-zero weather. Ice-cream seems one of the most popular Soviet dishes. The government has certainly tried hard to popularise it in recent years. It tasted considerably creamier than in Britain or America.

Clothes looked warm enough even for the Russian winter, but they were drab by comparison with those worn in European capitals. Looking down from a window on to a Moscow street, filled with crowds of people, mostly wearing black, all hurrying, reminded me of some Lancashire scene painted by Lowry.

I noticed that quite a few of the women wore stockings of some synthetic material resembling nylon. Mostly it was too cold for nylons, however. I soon changed to woollen stockings and wore them for the rest of the tour. But there appeared to be no nylon underwear or blouses—certainly I saw none in any of my window-shopping—and there was almost no make-up used except for a little lipstick. Exceptions were the Moscow dancers, who used make-up fairly freely.

The cold resulted in Jhana turning up in a splendidly cut pair of slacks on the morning we left for our tour. I was amused because she had obviously thought a great deal about whether she should do this and was most anxious about our reactions. Did we mind? Were we shocked? Did women wear slacks in public in the West? I reassured her on all these points, and she wore them most days during our trip.

There were not very many cars in the streets, even in Moscow, and we saw almost no motor-cycles or cycles. But probably the

77

cold weather was responsible for the latter being laid-up for the winter. People travelled in the cities chiefly by bus, trolley-bus, tram, and underground. We did not see a cat or a dog the whole time we were in Moscow, and not very many outside the capital.

But we did see masses of healthy-looking children. The approach to children was one of the most attractive things about the Russians. I have said that people were always warmly clad. It was interesting to note, though, that whatever the clothes of the parents, the child's usually were just a little better and a little more colourful.

Children do seem to have a more important place in Russia than in the West. Always there is talk of the future, and the children who will be the future. This, reinforced with the traditional Russian attitude towards the family, means that the young are given every possible attention, though somehow the parents do not seem to spoil them.

Their feeling about children even came out in their speeches of welcome, in which they always mentioned Ingvar. This was a touch which always made me melt inside, for, of course, Sven and I were constantly missing him.

Television, as in Britain, is playing a more and more important part in the life of the average Russian. There is already a second programme in Moscow—though not, of course, a commercial one! —and one of our abiding memories is the clusters of TV aerials bristling from every house and block of flats.

The fact that even small houses usually had several aerials spotlighted two of the most important social factors in present-day Russia—the increase in the supply of consumer goods contrasted with the continuance of terrible overcrowding. The Russians all admit that their bad housing is their major problem, and I was certainly shaken by some of the evidence of this.

There is more ballet on Russian TV than in England, as one would expect from a country where it is so much more popular. There are also numerous ballet clubs, and quite a large number of amateur ballet companies, who occupy about the same position there that amateur dramatic and amateur operatic societies have in Britain.

I don't expect to see such enthusiasm for ballet here for many years, and it is obvious from what I have written that I feel we have much to learn from the Russians. But that is not to say that I came home despondent about our own art. Quite the reverse.

I am, in fact, filled with hope about the future. The Russians have had so much longer than we have had to learn, to develop, and to appreciate. The true history of British ballet hardly spans my own lifetime. But though I would not pretend that we can yet equal their achievements, already the names of British dancers are famous all over the world. Certainly our ballet is considered by most second only to Russia's.

My own experience was surely heartening. I did not know how I was going to be received. I don't think that the Russians were quite certain what they were going to get! So, how encouraging it was, after a short time there, to find that I was being considered seriously by them—that I was not a freak, an eccentricity from foggy England, but a serious colleague. I was genuinely thrilled to find that they were as interested in me as I was in them.

Their whole attitude was one of interest in British dancing. They knew the names of all our great figures. They were as eager to hear about them as we are to hear about Ulanova and her colleagues.

Now the exchange is continuing. Last spring Madame Bocharnikova, the director of the Bolshoi Ballet School, was here in London looking at British dancing and training methods. Ballet is not a closed shop.

I hope that our art is one of the windows through which the Russians will be able to look at the Western world. What can the Russians see through this window? First, that there is much in the British character which is invaluable to any dancer. We have tenacity, sincerity, and an innate discipline with a feeling for poetry and lyricism. In carving out our future it is to be hoped that our ballet will reflect the British scene and character—not only of the present day but also of our great past, with its fine heritage in literature, music, and folklore.

And behind the dancers there is real enthusiasm from the public. Ballet does not yet hold the position it does in Russia, but in a very short time a surprisingly high appreciation of ballet has been developed. There is a large literature on the subject, and some excellent composers, designers, and critics of international rank, who have already given much to the world of ballet.

79

We can claim, too, that it is as difficult to get into the Royal Opera House in London as it is to get into the Bolshoi in Moscow. That is quite a thing to talk about in a nation which is believed by the outside world to be inartistic!

You queue for ballet tickets in London, of course, but there is not much queueing for them in Moscow. Seats are on sale roughly ten days ahead of performances. The biggest queues are at the excellent Bolshoi cloakrooms, where it is obligatory to leave one's coat, hat, and snow galoshes before being allowed into the theatre.

Bolshoi tickets have to be booked in advance unless you belong to some organisation, such as a trade union, which is allocated blocks of seats, or unless you are a diplomat or a foreign visitor, when it is fairly easy to get in.

Personally, I got the impression that the Bolshoi audience, despite the importance of the company, was not so regular a public as those outside the capital. It may be that the system of allocating Bolshoi seats produces a more deserving or a more cosmopolitan audience than in Tiflis, Kiev, or Leningrad, but it does not seem to produce such a discerning ballet audience.

Russian audiences, generally, are obviously used only to the highest standards in music as well as dancing. In giving a performance one senses that they are a musical people. They are also fascinated by spectacle, and my experiences in *Giselle* showed also how they like theatrical stage effects.

They applaud really fiercely when they are pleased. There is no half-heartedness and their clapping is loud and long. An encouraging feature of their applause is the way in which large numbers of people leave their seats at the end, and advance down the aisles in quite an orderly way to the orchestra pit, where they stand clapping vigorously and calling out their praise. I was also happy to notice that a majority of the orchestra usually stayed behind at the end and stood up to applaud.

Another difference is in curtain-calls. When I sat in the director's box and watched a Bolshoi performance for the first time, I looked carefully to see what the custom was in Russia. Plisetskaya took three curtain calls at the end—a procedure which is equivalent to about a dozen in Britain.

Watching her, I learnt the etiquette. After calls with the full

80

company the curtains close, and you are pushed out front between them. You curtsy. Then you walk miles and miles over to the left side of the stage, reverence, return to the centre, and repeat the whole thing to the right. When you return to the centre for the third time, with the audience and orchestra still shouting, your partner invariably kisses your hand before you retire with a final bow. This ceremony is repeated for each call.

The fans are most demonstrative. They loaded me with gifts whenever I danced. If anything, they are more numerous outside Moscow than in the capital. Although they crowd round stage-doors like their opposite numbers all over the world, they tend to be more formal about their presents, and ring up to ask if they can see the artist personally.

When I saw any of them in my hotel I used to offer them some small hospitality in return for their presents. But it was always hard to get them to accept even the smallest pastry, for example, though they were delighted once they had taken the first bite. I found this attitude constantly and put it down to the fact that the Russians take chief pride in being hosts.

Yuri had one particularly devoted fan who used to follow him as much as possible. She came to see us—or, rather, him—dance in Leningrad. He used to have his leg pulled about one occasion when he was just going to fly off to some distant part of the Soviet Union and was actually in his seat, with the engines turning. Then there was a great commotion and the aeroplane door opened and in burst Yuri's fan. She had come to offer her good wishes and, although late, was determined to speak to him before the plane left! That is one of the amusing stories I brought back from Russia. But I also brought back serious memories of the wonderful way in which I had been received by Soviet dancers. I should love to go back there again. I should love, also, to dance with Yuri again, either in his country or in mine.

What did my journey achieve? Well, it certainly interested the Russians. They, as one of the oldest ballet countries, wanted to see a ballerina from one of the newest ones. But the visit also helped me. I learned much while I was there. I had reached the end of one road with the Royal Ballet. My dancing with the Russians started me on another one.

I dare to hope my visit did a little good to relations between our two countries. I know it did no harm. It certainly reinforced my belief that the more the people of one country see the art and the artists of another, the more they will realise the many things they have in common.

If I could sum up my visit in one sentence, it would not be in my words but in those of the ballet mistress at Leningrad who introduced herself by saying: "I can't speak English but we have a common language." I was very proud to go to Russia and speak that language in my English accent.

# INDEX

83

Lightning Source UK Ltd.
Milton Keynes UK
UKHW020651150223
417035UK00008B/155